Cambridge Proficiency
Examination Practice 3

Teacher's Book

Cambridge Proficiency Examination Practice 3

Teacher's Book

University of Cambridge Local Examinations Syndicate

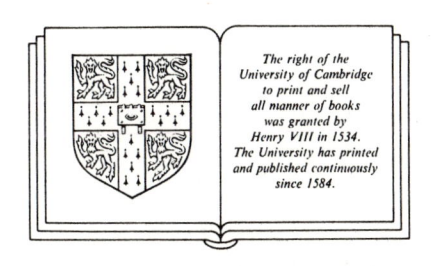

Cambridge University Press
Cambridge
New York   Port Chester
Melbourne   Sydney

Published by the Press Syndicate of the University of Cambridge
The Pitt Building, Trumpington Street, Cambridge CB2 1RP
40 West 20th Street, New York, NY 10011, USA
10 Stamford Road, Oakleigh, Melbourne 3166, Australia

© Cambridge University Press 1990

First published 1990
Reprinted 1990

Printed in Great Britain at The Bath Press, Avon

ISBN 0 521 36778 6 Teacher's Book
ISBN 0 521 36777 8 Student's Book
ISBN 0 521 36600 3 Set of 2 cassettes

Copyright
The law allows a reader to make a single copy of part of a book
for purposes of private study. It does not allow the copying of
entire books or the making of multiple copies of extracts. Written
permission for any such copying must always be obtained from the
publisher in advance.

BS

Contents

Introduction 1

The Certificate of Proficiency Examination 2

Practice Test 1 17

Practice Test 2 30

Practice Test 3 44

Practice Test 4 58

Practice Test 5 72

Optional Reading 86

Publisher's note
For details of sources of illustrations and other copyright material, please see the Student's Book.

Introduction

The tests in *Cambridge Proficiency Examination Practice 3* are designed to familiarise students with the style and format of the Certificate of Proficiency in English (CPE) examination papers and to provide them with practice in examination techniques. The tests can be used in class for pre-examination practice and discussion, as 'mock examinations', or by students working alone using the Teacher's Book as a key. The tests are reproduced exactly as they appear in the examination.

A suggested mark scheme for each of the tests is provided in the Teacher's Book, but it must be emphasised that no fully authoritative assessment of students can be based on this. In the CPE examination itself a series of complex statistical procedures is carried out to correlate a candidate's performance in all five papers, and such procedures cannot be accurately reproduced by the teacher working alone.

The current CPE examination syllabus was introduced in 1975 and modified in 1984. Broadly speaking, there are four different ideas underlying the syllabus:
a) the now universal acceptance of communicative approaches in the EFL classroom, which is reflected in and, indeed, encouraged by the CPE examination;
b) the increased prominence of listening and speaking skills in classrooms, reflected in greater weighting in the examination;
c) the view that reading and listening texts should be taken from authentic sources within a candidate's range of experience, and not be specially written, abridged or over-literary;
d) the need to avoid culture bias in the examination, confirming the status of English as an international language.

The ways in which these ideas are embodied in the examination itself are outlined on pages 2 to 14 and can be seen in the practice tests in the Student's Book.

The Teacher's Book contains:
– a suggested mark scheme and answer key for each paper;
– complete transcripts of the recorded Listening Comprehension tests;
– instructions on the handling of the Interview tests.

The two accompanying cassettes contain the recordings for the Listening Comprehension tests. The tests cannot be used without the appropriate cassette.

The Certificate of Proficiency Examination

The chart below gives an outline of how each paper of the CPE examination is assessed. In the examination the final assessment of any candidate is reached only on the basis of total performance in all five papers and after the marks have been carefully correlated and adjusted to establish correct weightings and grading levels. Adjustments are also made to offset the effect of random guessing in multiple-choice and true/false questions. Such procedures are clearly impracticable for the teacher working alone. However, the information in the chart below and throughout this book can be used as a guide to an approximate assessment of a candidate's likely level of performance.

The complete examination carries a total of 180 marks.

Name of paper	Time	Total marks	Assessment
Paper 1 Reading Comprehension	1 hour	40	A mark contributing to a pass grading in the whole examination is normally about 60% of the possible score for this paper.
Paper 2 Composition	2 hours	40	An impression mark is given, following a grading scale for each composition. On average, pass candidates score about 40% of the paper total and very good candidates 75–90%.
Paper 3 Use of English	2 hours	40	This paper is marked according to a detailed mark scheme. On average, pass candidates score 50–60% of the paper total.
Paper 4 Listening Comprehension	about 30 minutes	20	This paper is marked according to a detailed mark scheme with varied weighting for items. On average, pass candidates score about 60% of the paper total.
Paper 5 Interview	15 to 20 minutes	40	An impression mark is given on six grading scales. On average, pass candidates score about 60% of the paper total.

The Certificate of Proficiency

Paper 1: Reading Comprehension (1 hour)

Paper 1 is in two sections: Section A with 25 multiple-choice questions, each consisting of a sentence with a blank to be filled by one of four words or phrases, and Section B with 15 multiple-choice questions on two or more reading passages.

Section A tests candidates' knowledge of English vocabulary (including synonyms, antonyms, collocations and phrasal verbs) as well as their knowledge of grammatical rules and constraints.

Section B tests candidates' general understanding of the gist of passages as well as their understanding of specific information given. Some questions also test appreciation of stylistic effects, nuance and register. The passages vary in length, character and density and are drawn from a variety of authentic sources, including fiction, non-fiction, newspapers, magazines, brochures, leaflets and advertisements.

Marking

Section A carries a total possible mark of 25; the 15 questions in Section B count **double**. An incorrect answer gains no mark, but no marks are specifically deducted for wrong answers. The final 'raw' total of 55 is scaled down to a maximum of 40.

Exam preparation

It is important not to practise this type of test to excess, but merely to accustom students to its requirements and tempo. Multiple-choice questions have more value as a testing device than as a teaching method and excessive practice in doing this type of test is unlikely to improve students' ability to read English more efficiently. Time should be devoted in class, therefore, to improving students' reading skills and not just their ability to answer reading comprehension questions.

Students should be given experience of reading authentic texts of the kind shown in *Cambridge Proficiency Examination Practice 3* and given help in learning how to understand them. Such help may include teaching students how to understand the gist of a passage and how to extract the main points of information from it without necessarily understanding every single word they read.

Paper 2: Composition (2 hours)

Two compositions, of the varying word length specified, are to be written in the two hours allotted. The choice of topics includes (at the full 350-word length) a descriptive, a discursive and a narrative topic, a shorter more specific topic or an exercise based on a specific task (250–300 words) and a topic (of 350 words) based on optional reading as specified in the examination Regulations for each year. The advantage for candidates of choosing to read one of the three texts selected for the exam is that it may offer them an enjoyable and worthwhile reading experience, with an opportunity to develop the ability to handle ideas and literary themes in English, as well as a wider range of topics to choose from in Paper 2. Candidates may also have the chance to discuss their reading in the Interview (see page 12).

The Certificate of Proficiency Examination

Marking

An impression mark out of 20 is given for each composition, using the scale shown below. This mark is based on an overall impression of the language used, including the range and appropriateness of vocabulary, sentence and paragraph structure and correctness of grammar, spelling and punctuation. Individual mistakes are not penalised. The language used should be, for a pass grade and above, at a level of fluency, accuracy and resource appropriate to the Proficiency examination, reflected also in the relevance and organisation of each composition as a whole and in terms of individual preparation.

Language rather than content is the main concern in the marking, since a candidate's general command of the language shows in the attempt to communicate some personal interest in the topic. Marks are not taken off for unorthodox opinions, illogical arguments or lack of special creativity in selecting and developing descriptive detail.

The task-directed exercise is intended to reveal sensitivity to features of style appropriate to the English used for various special purposes, and ability to reproduce these features appropriately.

The topics on the three books are also task-directed, in the sense that they require ability to recall and marshal facts and themes from the text studied in the framework of the question set. Detailed factual recall is not a crucial factor in the marking, nor is training in the technique of literary analysis, the emphasis being, as with the other topics, on the quality of language used in response to the given stimulus.

For all topics, the inclusion of irrelevant material which seems to have been learnt by heart does lose marks. Over-short compositions will lose marks, as may over-long ones because they often contain more mistakes or are badly structured.

	Language	*Content*	*Background Texts*
16–20	Ambitious in concept and approach, with high quality language use. Occasional native-speaker-type lapses.		13–20 Interpretative in approach. Credit given for breadth, development and relevance of argument, appropriateness of illustration and quotation.
11–15	Natural and appropriate in style with only occasional errors. Some sophistication of language use.	Well-developed realisation of the task.	
8–10	Structure and usage communicated in a clear but limited manner.	Task reasonably attempted.	8–12 Limited to a straightforward narrative treatment. Credit given for clarity, organisation, and appropriate selection of material.
5–7	Lack of control/numerous errors.	Topic area neither extended nor explored.	1–7 Irrelevant, undirected and fails to demonstrate knowledge or understanding of the text.
1–4	Errors and narrowness of vocabulary prevent communication.	Gross irrelevance and/or too short for judgement to be formed.	

The following sample compositions taken from the Syndicate's reports illustrate the quality of language which typifies candidates in all but the lowest of the categories indicated above.

17 MARKS
Describe someone who has greatly influenced your life and explore the reasons for this influence.

Before anything else I think I have to describe the circumstances of my life. My parents are divorced and I have never lived together with my real father because when the divorce happened I was about one year old. At my age of ten my mother had a boyfriend. The better she knew him the more he spent the time with us. So the things developed and now we are living together. For me he is like my father. He is the person who has influenced my life and to a certain extent my character.

My father or let's call him Peter has a strong character. He knows exactly what he wants and I assume therefore he is very successful in business. He owns a company which sell fire engines and vehicles. Through his profession he became very decisive and strict. But he is also very kind and warm-hearted. If I have a problem I know I can go to him and he'll find time to listen to me. That gives me somehow a good and sound feeling. My father has dark hair and is very tall which gives you the impression of a respectful person. What I like mostly are his eyes. They seem to me like little laughing bowls.

There are a lot of reasons for his influence on me. At the beginning it wasn't easy for him and me to accept each other. The greatest problem for me was the fact that suddenly I have to share my mother with somebody else. But exactly this difficulty changed my character. I learnt to accept another person in our house and through that I wasn't always the centre of my mother's attention. Peter gave me in a way some of my independence. In addition to that change Peter showed me a lot in his company. Last but not least he did and does influence me sometimes by discussions we have. I see his point of view which is quite interesting and sometimes different from mine.

In conclusion I would like to mention that Peter helped me a lot as far as my personal development concerns. I think I learnt and I will learn a lot of him. I am really grateful to have met him and to know such a wonderful person.

Examiner's comments:
This is a very well-developed essay which flows naturally to a satisfactory conclusion. A few mistakes or infelicities of expression prevent the composition falling into the upper half of this category.

14 MARKS
Write a story which begins or ends: "Home at last!"

"Home at last" sighed George, as the cab turned round the final corner before his house. Jenny, his wife, was asleep, and his little son Gregory wasn't paying any attention. After a disastrous week in France, however, 'home at last' was all George had been wanting to say for days.

The ferry trip over to Calais was uneventful. As soon as they had settled into the hotel however, things had started to go from bad to worse. The snails they had eaten on their first day had played havoc with all of their stomachs. In fact they hadn't left their hotel room for three days.

On the fourth day, their hopes of going to the beach were shattered by the weather. For the next three days it seemed as little as a summer holiday as it possibly could, but six days inside a hotel room were nothing compared to what happened on their trip home.

The ferry back to Dover was delayed by five hours. In eventually setting foot on English soil again, Jenny swore she would never go to France again. Gregory had become very pale on the ferry-trip back, but was now back to normal. They had decided to leave the car at a special parking lot in Dover, from where they now picked it up. On the motorway, with little other cars around, and especially not a garage to be seen, the car had promptly broken down.

The Automobile Association had said it would take about a week to repair their car. The damage was very serious, they had said. The family then took the bus which would have taken them quite near their house. However, six-year-old Gregory's stomach finally couldn't take it any longer, and he was sick in the bus just half an hour later.

Eventually, being very near their house, they took a cab in which Jenny fell asleep. As they neared their street George sighed "Home at last!" Jenny mumbled something that sounded like "All we need now is to have been broken into." But George wasn't listening. He was looking at their half-opened front door.

Examiner's comments:
This is a well-organised story, free from basic errors; a story line is developed, with quite effective expression.

The Certificate of Proficiency

13 MARKS

Basing your answer on your reading of the prescribed text concerned, answer the following:
Anita Brookner: Hotel du Lac
Edith Hope's relationships with men are the most important aspects of the novel. Discuss.

David Simmonds is a married man and, according to Edith's theory of a Tortoise and a hair he would probably be the latter – successful in his work, as well as in social life, he had nothing for Edith to offer. He was her lover and she was his 'last resort'. Edith loved him dearly – she used to cook him meals and pretended they were a family whenever they were together. David wasn't a demanding partner and that provided enough space for Edith's vivid imagination. David became a symbol of what Edith expected from 'her man' – she imagined he was her friend and wrote him many letters from Hotel du Lac, without sending them, of course.

Geoffrey Long was friendly, calmed person who lacked self confidence after his mother had died and expected to have a proper, settled marriage. Edith let him down and made him "look like a laughing stock" – the worst insult couldn't have been made to him. He was hurt and therefore didn't understand Edith's reaction. He was just as ordinary as anybody else among her 'so-called' friends. That certainly couldn't suit Edith's character.

In my opinion, Philip Neville was the most interesting mail character in the book. He was very elegant, refine, good-humoured, intelligent and he wasn't married. He had offered a marriage which sounded like a business deal and did fit Edith's general idea of independancy but was unacceptable in terms of love and feelings. Edith didn't want to marry a man who would treat her like a piece of antique expensive furniture.

Nevile seems as if he embodies David and Geoffrey at the same time – David, becouse he's attractiv, he's successful, with a strong will and a friendly approach to her intellect. On the other hand, Neville would marry Edith for the same reason as Geoffrey wanted – to settle down, to help his 'ego' feel better, to gain a normal (and orthodox) social position and to fulfil the emptiness made by another woman (a mother in Geoffrey's case and a wife in Mr Nevill's).

Neville as such, was the last temptation as well as the last chance for Edith. By rejecting it, Edith has decided to be herself.

Examiner's comments:
The language is slightly below the range of the 11–13 category but the answer is imaginative, shows assurance and handles the theme very effectively.

12 MARKS

Your friends have accepted an invitation to come and stay in your house while you and your family are away. Write a letter giving them all the information necessary to make their visit enjoyable and trouble-free.

1333 Bolton Road
Pelham, Manor, N.Y.
10803
(USA)

Mary Anne Jones
30–14 42nd Street
Astoria, Queens, 1
11103
USA

Dear Mary,
   Hi! Hope my letter finds you all healthy and well. As you can see summer is here and my trip to France is just a few days away. My family and I will leave on the 14th so you can 'move in' for the summer on the 15th.
   I really hope your stay at my house will be enjoyable, trouble-free and worthwhile.
   Well, as you know the house has 4 double bedrooms and a master bedroom. You could use any of the four but I'd prefer not having mum's room used. There is plenty of space for your clothes in the closets and you can put your luggage under the bed. Sheets, covers, nightgowns, are clean and in the

wardrobe. Oh, by the way. John can use my brother's room and Mike, Dan's (since they are boys).
    You can use my stereo, my video and of course the television to have fun at night. My records are in the lower, left cuboard and the videocassetes are on the right shelf.
    If you want to read, help yourself to the books which are in the library.
    The refrigarator is full of food. If you need any more you can shop at the supermarket.
    The mixer is near the fridge and all the pots and pans in the cuboard next to the stove.
    Plates, nives, glasses are in the dishwasher and in the cuboard above the sink.
    Towels, soap, sponges are in the bamboo basket in the bathroom.
    Help yourselves to anything available in the house. Have lots of fun. Hope to see you soon.

    Love
        Ellie

P.S. The keys are in the mailbox.
We'll be back on August 15.

Examiner's comments:
Plenty of sensible information is given; the language is simple, but chatty and appropriate in style.

10 MARKS

There is a saying: 'Money can't buy happiness, but it can help!' Do you agree?

In a swirling gray world my brother felt compelled to make a decision. It was as if there was light and commotion on one side, darkness and quiteness on the other. He chose the light. And life. He was in the hospital after a car accident. The doctors gently suggested to my parents that John – my brother – would have to live in a wheelchair as his back was broken. . . . I have always thought that there was a protective shield around my family. My parents were supportive, my grandfather always there to rely on. Grandfather was a very rich man and some day my brother and I would succeed to the property. Although I have never thought that money is of any real value, I was aware of the fact that wealthy people are better off. At the age of 18 I had my own car, a popular and expensive model, I was exorbitantly extravagant and I have travelled a lot.
    But now, under those circumstances, money counted for little. No matter how rich my family was, my brother would spend all his life sitting in a wheelchair. Could money compensate a young man for his paralysed body? Would money be of any real help when John would have to struggle to live as a paraplegic?
I do not suggest that money doesn't make your life easier. What I suggest is that when confronted with illness and death only God can help you. Of course you may argue: ''rich people can afford being treated at expensive clinics. Others not.'' Although rich can lead a much easier life, I have a feeling that fate always has some blows in store for them.
    On the other hand, money ensures a better education for you, if that's what you want. Someone else is doing the cleaning and cooking and ironing for you. You can afford travelling abroad, expensive hotels, nice restaurants.
    But I know dozens of people who went through life and met their goals without being rich and more important, without the underlying aim of becoming rich. They had only confidence in their ability to cope with difficulties. They did acknowledge that money can help. Nevertheless, they were aware of so many other things that can help anyone to lead an interesting and fulfilling life. Is it any wonder that these people are the happiest?

Examiner's comments:
This is quite a well-organised essay; the ideas are expressed reasonably well and the level of accuracy is just acceptable for Proficiency level.

9 MARKS

Describe someone who has greatly influenced your life and explore the reasons for this influence.

My grandparents have greatly influenced my life for many reasons. I think they have brought a lot to my personality and my conception of life.
    My grandparents brought me up. When I was a child, as both my father and my mother worked, my

The Certificate of Proficiency

grandparents used to mind me. I have quite good memories of that period. I remember that, as a child, it was fun to live in the countryside and to play with the cats, the chickens or the rabbits my grandparents had. It was fun to play in the little stream near the house or to go for walks in the woods or in the fiels and make bunches of flowers. Apart from the happiness and the care they provided me with, my grandparents also taught me certain fundamental values. The values that are so vivid in the countryside, where people know each others and talk to each others.

Personally, I believe that a lot of my personality is connected with my early years spent with my grandparents. They have influenced my life, that is my way of life. They led a very simple life, one of those lives that is described as 'close to nature'. They respected nature and their neighbours and they had this sense of shareness that nowadays, in our advanced societies, does not mean anything any longer. They still believed in Mankind and in God. Their faith in God was a very strong one and, at home, we used to celebrate Christmas, Eastern . . . Every Sunday morning, we used to go to church and there was no work allowed on Sundays!

I believe my grandparents have influenced me the way any grandparents influence any little girl or boy. However, the fact that they lived in the countryside is very important and accounts for a lot of their beliefs and for my feelings when I remember those days.

All in all, I must acknowledge that they have greatly influenced my life because of the values, the ideas, the love for nature, the faith in a religion they have brought me up with.

Examiner's comments:
The ideas are communicated clearly and there are few errors, but the style is elementary.

7 MARKS
'A sense of humour is the most important of all human qualities.' Do you agree?

I should say that a sense of humour is really important in every person, even essential sometimes but not the most important quality of a person.

First of all, it's common knowledge that nowadays people tend to be very worried and distressed due to the many difficulties they have to face in the actual everyday life and everybody knows as well that the more worried people become more difficult will be to find the solutions to their problems and that a sense of humour is essential in this kind of experience. But which also has to be considered is that is not so easy to a person who is facing any kind of problem which is disturbing his life, to have a sense of humour and besides that they need someone who helps them in this part of their lives, some good advices, someone to talk freely about their problems and not a person who has a great sense of humour and is joking all the time because if it happens, the person who has the problem will think that the other is not taking him serious.

So, if a person has an easy sense of humour and can cope with her problems with no dificulties it's very nice but that's not what happens with the great majority. There's a great mixture of feelings in a human being and sometimes is difficult to balance them and it varies from person to person, while a person thinks that his sense of humour will always help them to face his life, another person thinks that it is important, but not always and sometimes it can even turn things more difficult.

Many things have to be considered when dealing with people's feelings and as I mentioned before a sense of humour is important to make life sometimes easier and happier but it is not the most important quality of a person. What is worthy when someone has a great sense of humour but is unable to help another person who needs his help in another way. It would work fine if easier to be found and if suited everybody.

Examiner's comments:
Several statements are unclear but the candidate does have some ideas. There is an acceptable shape to the argument but it falls apart because of lack of language control. The language is *not* Proficiency level.

5 MARKS
You have recently received a number of comments from local residents, some of which are printed below. As representative of the local committee of residents, write a letter to the authorities outlining people's concerns and suggesting what should be done.

"They throw bottles into my garden and tear up my plants!"
"Teenagers roam in gangs and I get frightened!"
"The streets are dirty and full of litter!"
"The walls are covered with graffiti!"
"The public telephone's always broken!"
"Young hooligans race on motor bikes round the square!"

                                                      56 Hartington Grove
                                                      Cambridge

Public Authorities Government   14 June 1989
119 Mill Road
Cambridge

Dear Sir,

First of all, I am writing this letter to say something as a representative of local committee of residents. I hope you will consider about it.

Secondly I am telling you about some residents claim. To tell you the truth, I was surprised that I received so many comments from local residents. And their comments are both private matters and public matters. As for private matters, one of them was destroyed her garden by someone throwing bottles. Nowadays gardening is a very popular hobby and people love their plants very much. I can understand her mind. Another comment was that she was frightened of teenager because they were roaming in gangs. I know the problem of children's delinquence is very difficult. But you must find out the solution because you are responsible for it. And one more comment concerned with private matters was that young people were doing hooligans race on motor bikes round the square. This is also concerned with children's deliquence. But in my opinion they don't realise how dangerous that game is until someone injure seriously.

Next, as for public matters, their comments were about litter in the streets and graffiti on the walls and the public telephone which were always broken.

Thirdly, I would like to suggest what you should do to solve our problems. I know it is very difficult to solve these kind of things. Some people are still unemployment and it follows that every person doesn't have enough money to make a living. In my opinion level of people's living should be improved more and more. And I would like you to make great efforts for it.

Finally, I hope you will consider our problems and I am glad you will pay attention to my suggestion.

Faithfully yours,

Examiner's comments:
This candidate has very poor control of the language and only just communicates.

Exam preparation

Students should be given practice in writing compositions on all the different types of topics at the required length and within the time available (about one hour). They should be trained to develop the skill of using language appropriate to different types of writing. This training should include exercises based on specific tasks. In the case of candidates intending to choose in the actual exam one of the topics based on optional reading, suitable practice questions should be devised for them to discuss and write about, based on the current syllabus (published in the Regulations each year). Questions of this type are included in *Cambridge Proficiency Examination Practice 3* for practice by students who may have worked on these books in class.

The Certificate of Proficiency

Paper 3: Use of English (2 hours)

This paper has two sections: Section A contains exercises to test the candidate's active control of English usage and grammatical structure, while Section B consists of a number of questions testing comprehension and skill in summarising, based on a passage. The range of these exercises is illustrated in *Cambridge Proficiency Examination Practice 3*.

Marking

Detailed mark schemes, based on a maximum mark of 80, with Section A carrying about 45 marks and Section B about 35, are given in this book for each of the five Use of English papers. (The 'raw' maximum of 80 is scaled down to a weighted total of 40.)

Exam preparation

It should be noted that many of the exercises in Section A have more value as testing devices than as classroom exercises. Too much emphasis on such exercises in class may not increase students' language awareness or communicative skills. In particular, the modified cloze test (Question 1) should not be over-practised in class.

In preparing for Section B, students should be given practice in reading a wide range of texts from different sources and in answering questions on information given or implied and the language used. They should also practise summarising the information presented in texts, using their own words as far as possible and avoiding direct quotation.

Paper 4: Listening Comprehension (about 30 minutes)

A cassette recording is played to candidates while they complete an answer sheet. Candidates listen to three or four authentic or simulated authentic texts, complete with all necessary spoken instructions; each text is normally heard twice on the cassette.

The texts include broadcasts, conversations, discussions, announcements and telephone calls, with speakers using both standard and non-standard speech styles. The questions include reordering or matching information, labelling and blank-filling, as well as multiple-choice and true/false questions. The questions test candidates' ability to extract information from the texts, to interpret the speakers' attitudes or intentions and to recognise the implications of stress and intonation patterns.

Marking

The final total of 20 marks (which involves the adjustment of raw scores to allow for appropriate weighting parity between test versions and to offset the guessing factor in multiple-choice or true/false questions) gives, together with Paper 5, one third of the total marks in the examination. A complete mark scheme is given in this book for each of the five Listening Comprehension papers.

Exam preparation

Students should become accustomed to the form and tempo of the recordings used in the examination. In particular, they should be exposed to recordings of speakers using unsimplified English, spoken at a natural speed. They should realise that understanding spoken English involves extracting the main points of information from a text and does not necessarily depend on understanding every word that is spoken. Classroom practice using task-based exercises is recommended.

Many of the recordings used in these practice tests and in the examination itself are taken from BBC World Service broadcasts. Wherever possible, students should be encouraged to listen to BBC World Service broadcasts in English. (Details can be obtained from the BBC, Bush House, London WC2B 4PH, or from any British Council office.)

This Teacher's Book contains transcripts of the recordings used in *Cambridge Proficiency Examination Practice 3*. These are included only to help teachers handle the tests confidently and see what each piece is about and how long it lasts. The transcripts should *not* be used to help students to 'spot the answers' to the questions. Many questions depend on interpreting what is heard on the cassette, including the stress and intonation of the speakers which cannot be shown in a transcript.

Note: The recordings of the two cassettes that accompany *Cambridge Proficiency Examination Practice 3* follow the format of the exam exactly. Each text is heard twice with 15 seconds of silence before and after each hearing, during which students can read through the questions or task and write down their answers. There are also full spoken instructions on the cassettes.

Paper 5: Interview (15 to 20 minutes)

The Interview consists of a theme-based conversation between the candidate and the examiner, or in the case of group interviews, among the candidates with occasional intervention by the examiner. Prompt material consisting of photographs, short passages, authentic texts and problem-solving activities are used to stimulate and guide the discussion. This form of syllabus incorporates developments made over a long period, notably the changes of 1984 which included increased weighting for the Interview, a change of format and an increased time allowance.

Candidates are assessed on overall performance in the tasks set by marking scales related to six specific performance areas (see marking section on pages 12–14).

Provision is made for centres to opt for the Interview to be taken *either* in the usual candidate/examiner form *or* in groups of two or three candidates with an examiner. The added realism of a group Interview is strongly recommended, though this is treated as an option: arrangements in line with local preferences and administrative resources are made by individual examination centres. (Instructions will be issued by each centre accordingly.) The increased amount of 'candidate talking time' generated and reduction in 'examiner talking time' mean that group interviews can be accomplished relatively quickly and do not need to take proportionately longer than an examiner/candidate Interview. The examiner is thus also able to concentrate more on assessing the candidates and less on guiding (or leading) the conversation. In both the group and one-to-one format two examiners, one to act as assessor and one as interlocutor, may sometimes be used.

Procedure

The examiner's material consists of a number of 'packages' or theme-based sets of photographs and other prompts from which the complete Interview is conducted. The photographs have sets of suggested questions and follow-up topics, not all of which need be used. The conversation should move from specific commentary on the situation shown in the picture to associated themes, with the candidate encouraged to speak freely. Emphasis on the factual aspects of the photograph and questions based on identification of objects and vocabulary are avoided. It should be remembered that it is the candidate's language skills that are being tested, not their personality, intelligence or knowledge of the world.

The candidate is then given a few moments to look through a passage before being asked to discuss its probable source and intention and its relation to the general theme of discussion. Full reading aloud of the passage is not normally required, but candidates may quote from it where this is appropriate to the discussion.

The Interview is completed either by a discussion of a piece of authentic material, for example, a leaflet, advertisement, extract from a newspaper or magazine, *and/or* a communicative activity using a variety of visual and verbal stimuli. The range of activities includes participation in a role-playing exercise, finding out information, giving and exchanging opinions, and problem-solving discussion. There is often an 'information gap' between the participants, leading to a realistic exchange of information and ideas between candidates (where the test is taken as a group) or between candidate and examiner.

The material includes some related to the optional background reading (see *Paper 2: Composition*). Provision is also being made in the Syndicate's current development work on oral testing for candidates to present project work as a basis for discussion during the Interview.

Cambridge Proficiency Examination Practice 3 contains five sample 'packages' of oral examiner's material (and one optional reading-based 'package'), which demonstrate the variety of passages and activity prompts used in the examination. Teachers may wish to prepare additional material (photographs, passages, realia) from other sources within the theme of each package to provide students with actual rather than copied material.

Marking

Candidates are marked by impression on different aspects of their spoken English throughout the Interview, as shown in the scales given below. The 'raw' maximum of 30 is scaled to a final total of 40. An adequate mark may be thought of as about 60% of the total available.

Similar marking scales are used in assessing both FCE and CPE candidates in the Interview. The main difference is that CPE candidates are expected to demonstrate that they are capable of producing longer stretches of clear, coherent speech and of performing well in more complex or more serious discussions. The material that is used is designed to give candidates the opportunity of demonstrating this ability.

It will be noticed that some of the activities in *Cambridge Proficiency Examination Practice 3* are based on fairly serious 'weighty' topics, such as famine or art, while others are based on more straightforward 'mundane' topics. Candidates at CPE level are expected to be able to discuss a wide variety of topics and to come closer to native-speaker competence than FCE candidates.

1 Fluency

- 5 Virtually native-speaker speed and rhythm in everyday contexts.
- 4 Minimal hesitation in all contexts.
- 3 Minimal hesitation in everyday contexts. Hesitation when discussing more abstract topics does not demand unreasonable patience of the listener.

- 2 Though hesitations not unreasonable in everyday contexts, would be trying the listener's patience with more abstract topics.
- 1 Hesitation frequent even in everyday contexts.
- 0 Not capable of connected speech.

2 Grammatical accuracy

- 5 Virtually native-speaker accuracy over a wide range of structures and in all contexts. Few if any errors of any kind.
- 4 Few errors even in complex structures when discussing abstract topics. No basic errors.
- 3 Structures adequately controlled and varied in most contexts. Few if any basic errors.

- 2 Structures adequate in everyday contexts but limited in range and with basic errors not infrequent.
- 1 Frequent basic errors.
- 0 No awareness of basic grammatical functions.

3 Pronunciation: Sentences

- 5 Virtually native-speaker stress-timing, rhythm, and placing of stress, intonation patterns and range of pitch within sentence; natural linking of phrases.
- 4 Stress-timing, rhythm, placing of stress, intonation etc. sufficiently native-like as to make comprehension easy and listening pleasurable.
- 3 Stress-timing, rhythm, placing of stress, intonation etc. sufficiently controlled.

- 2 Foreign speech patterns make the candidate occasionally difficult to understand.
- 1 Foreign speech patterns severely impede comprehension.
- 0 Not intelligible, through faulty stress and intonation.

4 Pronunciation: Individual sounds

- 5 All individual sounds virtually as a native speaker.
- 4 Most individual sounds virtually as a native speaker.
- 3 All sounds sufficiently correct, can be understood without difficulty.

- 2 Some individual sounds poorly articulated so that comprehension is sometimes difficult.
- 1 Individual sounds so poor that comprehension is often impossible.
- 0 Unintelligible.

5 Interactive communication

- 5 Wholly effective at communicating in all contexts.
- 4 Communicates effectively and with ease in most contexts, experiencing only occasional difficulty.
- 3 Communicates effectively and with ease in everyday contexts and adequately in more abstract contexts. Does not try the listener's patience.

- 2 Communication effective in everyday contexts but demands excessive patience in more abstract contexts.
- 1 Communicates poorly even in everyday contexts.
- 0 Communicates nothing.

6 Vocabulary resource

- 5 Wide-ranging, varied, precise and appropriate in all contexts.
- 4 Shows few vocabulary gaps other than in specialised areas. Rare need to paraphrase.
- 3 Adequate for all but specialised tasks, though paraphrase may sometimes be necessary.

- 2 Vocabulary though adequate for everyday tasks seldom rises above the mundane.
- 1 Lack of vocabulary makes performance even in everyday contexts inadequate.
- 0 Vocabulary too slight for communication at this level.

The Certificate of Proficiency

Exam preparation

Students should be encouraged at all times to do more than just 'answer questions' and to participate actively in a variety of communicative activities and discussions. Talking together in groups or in pairs is particularly valuable. Students may need special training in quick absorption of the relevant discussion content of passages and a variety of authentic material without attempting to puzzle out every word or background reference.

Note: The Student's Book of *Cambridge Proficiency Examination Practice 3* contains a selection of examination material (photographs, passages and prompts for communication activities) printed separately at the end of the book. This material is given in the Teacher's Book as Paper 5 in each practice test. Each interview paper is theme-related and has instructions for use. One 'package' based on a sample, set text is included in the Student's Book, after the theme-based Interview Exercises. Teacher's instructions for this are given on pages 86–8.

The University of Cambridge Local Examinations Syndicate have produced a video with accompanying notes in order to facilitate understanding of how group interviews are conducted. The video is available for purchase from:

EFL Department
University of Cambridge Local Examinations Syndicate
1, Hills Road
Cambridge CB1 2EU
United Kingdom

Practice Test 1

Paper 1: Reading Comprehension (1 hour)

Section A One mark for each correct answer.

1 B	6 D	11 A	16 C	21 C
2 B	7 A	12 B	17 A	22 C
3 D	8 A	13 B	18 A	23 C
4 C	9 C	14 B	19 B	24 B
5 D	10 A	15 A	20 A	25 A

Section B Two marks for each correct answer.

26 C	31 A	36 A
27 B	32 D	37 D
28 C	33 A	38 B
29 A	34 B	39 C
30 D	35 D	40 C

Total: 55

Paper 2: Composition (2 hours)

Give each composition a mark out of 20, according to the scale shown on page 4. If necessary, look at the sample compositions on pages 5–9 for further guidance on the standards required at each grade in the mark scheme.

Total: 40

Practice Test 1

Paper 3: Use of English (2 hours)

A complete mark scheme is given for each question. The 'raw' total of 78 for this paper would be adjusted to a mark out of 40 in the exam itself. Candidates passing the examination as a whole would be expected to score about 60% of the total marks.

Section A

Question 1   Give one mark for each correct answer.

1 as	8 rather	15 laid
2 into/to	9 in	16 into
3 such/interesting etc.	10 slow/restricted etc.	17 granted
4 from/since	11 as	18 first
5 first/earliest	12 anything	19 of/from
6 before	13 like	20 precede
7 chemical	14 less/fewer	

Total: 20

Question 2

Give one mark for each word or phrase between the vertical lines. Ignore the words printed in italics.

a) *If only* | your sister could come | *as well*.

b) *It looked* | as if/though the house had been | *unoccupied for several months.*

c) *Before these* | machines were invented | people had to queue. |

d) *He was too* | tired to stay awake | until the end | *of the film.*

e) *Norman's house may* | have been more expensive (than mine) but it is smaller and less attractive (than mine). |

f) *I was the* | last (person) to know about the accident. |

g) *Sarah's father said that if* | she had to go out | she should finish her homework first. |

h) *The soup powder* | just needs boiling water added to it | according to the instructions. |

Total: 12

Question 3

Give one mark for each correct word or phrase between the vertical lines. Ignore the words printed in italics.

a) *Only when he removed his dark glasses* | did I realise / could I see | who he was.

b) *Let's go home. There's* | no point / sense (in) | waiting any longer.

c) *After having had a chauffeur for so many years my brother took some time to* | (manage to) learn to drive | *himself.*

d) *If you had really wanted to succeed, you* | should / ought to have spent more | *time on your studies and less on playing games*.

e) *The more driving practice you have, the better chance you* | (will) have of passing | *your test*.

f) *He doesn't mind one way or the other; it makes* | no difference to | *him*.

Total: 6

Question 4

Give one mark for each word or phrase between the vertical lines, or two marks where shown. Ignore the words printed in italics.

a) *Be sure* | not to leave without saying goodbye | *to your grandmother*.

b) | I do not approve of | *that sort of behaviour*.

c) | The students did not take to their new lecturer. |

d) | There hasn't been a political scandal like this since the 1940's. |

e) | They do not let women into | *the inner temple*.

f) | They can't leave the dog behind when they go on holiday. | (2 marks)

g) | Don't come to / draw the conclusion | *that this job is easy*.

h) | (You must) Reduce (your) speed | *in town*.

Total: 9

Section B

Question 5

Give the mark shown for each question for coherent and relevant answers, not necessarily echoing the wording given here.

a) A person who used to smoke (1) wants to persuade others not to smoke (1). 2
b) (Idea that everyone must already know about the dangers of smoking.) 1
c) Having smoke blown in your face / being in the presence of smokers etc. 1
d) 'Born-again non-smokers' / people fighting against smoking etc. (1). Writer used to think they were busy-bodies etc. but now sees them as heroes, fighting against giant commercial interests (1). 2
e) The large tobacco manufacturing interests (1). (Mention of: unrestricted advertising / excessive power / limited / no opposition) (1). 2
f) Persuade new young customers to start smoking (1). (Idea that smoking kills and there is therefore a need by the manufacturers to find new smokers to stay in business (1).) 2
g) (Idea of concealment.) 1
h) Criticised/rebuked/told off etc. 1
i) People who buy shares in tobacco companies (1) without knowing that they have done this (1). 2
j) They took up smoking. 1

Practice Test 1

k) pusher = tobacco industry, addict = smoker (1). Pressure should be more on industry than on smoker (1).   2
l) A large company called Grand Met (1) nearly stopped its involvement with tobacco manufacturing (1).   2
m) The company directors' friends (1) could express disapproval of their involvement with the tobacco industry (dirty business etc.) (1).   2
n) Ten marks as follows:
   Difficulties – commercial interests (any two of): powerful companies, sports sponsorship, advertising, shareholders (2)
              – government interest (revenue) (1)   3
   Solutions – publicising names of holders of tobacco-related shares (1), encouraging big business pressure (1).   2
   Style – Subtract marks up to a total of 5 for: irrelevance, indiscriminate lifting and subjective comment (0–5).   5

Total: 31

Paper 4: Listening Comprehension (about 30 minutes)

First part: Mickleham

		Score
1	Tuesday	1
2	over 1000	1
3	50 years	1
4	in the last 5 years	1
5	not allowed/green belt	1
6	headmistress	1
7	1976	1
8	very happy/delighted	1
9	No	1
10	1844	1
11	Flower festival	1
12	(Marisa Robles)/concert	1
13	24th September	1

Total: 13 marks

Second part: Tie-man of the year

		Score
14	D	1
15	B	1
16	D	1
17	C	$\frac{1}{2}$

Total: $3\frac{1}{2}$ marks

Practice Test 1

Third part: Angela Blackstone

```
      Score
18 F   ½
19 F   ½
20 T   ½
21 F   ½
22 T   ½
23 F   ½
24 T   ½
      ___
```

Total: 3½ marks

Transcript

This is the Certificate of Proficiency Listening Comprehension Test.
Test Number 1
You will be given a question paper for the Certificate of Proficiency Test 1. Your supervisor will give you further instructions. On the question paper you will see spaces for your name and index number, and questions for each part of the test. Each part of the test will be heard twice. There will be pauses to allow you to look through the questions before each part, and other pauses to let you think about your answers. At the end of every pause you will hear this sound.

tone

The tape will now be stopped while question papers are given out. You must ask any questions now, as you will not be allowed to speak during the test.

pause

First part
You will hear a radio programme about a village called Mickleham. The interviewer has made some notes before the programme. Look at these notes on your question paper. As you listen to the programme, fill in the missing information in the spaces numbered 1 to 13. You are given two examples of what to write. You will hear the piece twice.

pause

tone

MICKLEHAM

Interviewer:	County World continues on County Sound with Tuesday's *Village Report* and tonight it's the turn of Mickleham and I've been joined by Mrs Mo Chisman and Mrs Gwynne Anderson from, well I suppose both of you from the village. Mo, may I start with you. Just exactly where is Mickleham?
Mo Chisman:	It's, um, on the old London road between Box Hill and Leatherhead.
Interviewer:	I must say it's a wonderful name, isn't it? Have I said that right?
Mo Chisman:	Mickleham, yes, that's right, yes.
Interviewer:	Do you know where the name comes from?
Mo Chisman:	Um, I, I think it derives from St Michael's Church which is just over a thousand years old.

Practice Test 1

Interviewer:	Ah, now I know you're not over a thousand years old. (*Oh, ha, ha*) How long have you been living there?
Mo Chisman:	Er, thirty years.
Interviewer:	Why did you choose to come there?
Mo Chisman:	Um, I married a man who, who lived in Mickleham and he's been there fifty years.
Interviewer:	Goodness. So have you seen many changes to the village?
Mo Chisman:	Oh, oh yes, quite a lot of changes, yes.
Interviewer:	In what respect?
Mo Chisman:	More so in the last five years than in previous years. Um, we've got Box Hill School there which has taken over the big house, er, one of the big houses in the area and, um, oh, people have changed. The, the old families have died out. A lot of new people have come in and it's just generally changed much, much as everywhere has changed really.
Interviewer:	Mm, yes, yes. Has there been any building going on?
Mo Chisman:	No, no, it's not allowed.
Interviewer:	Oh, I see. All right. Well, perhaps we ought to bring in Gwynne at this point, because I know you're headmistress of the Mickleham School, St Michael's Mickleham school. Gwynne, how long have you been doing that?
Gwynne Anderson:	I've, uh, been there since 1976.
Interviewer:	And why did you choose to come there? Was it an area that you knew well or what?
Gwynne Anderson:	Well, I live in Bookham and, um, I taught actually in Bookham schools and Leatherhead schools and you see I knew of Mickleham and I was absolutely delighted to be offered the appointment.
Interviewer:	Oh, yes. Is it like a village school? Where do most of the children come from?
Gwynne Anderson:	Well, there has been a change in the school population actually due to the change of the – well, there are no longer many big estates and households and in the past the children of the estate workers used to come to the village school but now you see, well, there's been a decrease in the population in Mickleham and an increase in the population in Box Hill (*Oh yes*.) so our catchment area is now Box Hill and, um, some children from Mickleham, oh, and a few from West Humble.
Interviewer:	Mm, mm. So how old is the school itself?
Gwynne Anderson:	Oh, there's been a school continuously in Mickleham since, er, 1844.
Interviewer:	Goodness. Now, Mo, perhaps we can come back to you finally. I know there's a couple of things coming up that you'd like to mention.
Mo Chisman:	Er, yes. Yes. There's, there's a flower festival at Mickleham Church on Saturday 1st October, so that's Saturday, and Sunday and, um, we have Marisa Robles giving a concert on the 1st October in the church. She's been before and it's a beautiful concert and tickets are available and they're £3.50, and the Horticultural Show on September 24th.
Interviewer:	Lovely, so a few things happening there. Mo, Gwynne, many thanks indeed for coming into County Sound and chatting about Mickleham. I wish you a safe journey home. (*Oh, thank you.*) It's a bit miserable out there, but I'll play you a nice record. Here's Paul Young ...

pause

tone

Now you will hear the piece again. [*The piece is repeated.*]

pause

That is the end of the first part of the test.

pause

Second part
You will now hear another radio programme in which the interviewer asks a man about his choice of ties. As you listen to the programme, answer questions 14 to 17. You must tick one of the boxes A, B, C or D to show the correct answer. You will hear the piece twice.

pause

tone

TIE-MAN OF THE YEAR

Presenter:	Every year, the British Clothing Industry Federation names a Tie-man of the Year, chosen, as you might expect, by the neckties he wears throughout the year. This year's Tie-man is Trinidadian Trevor Macdonald, British television's only black male newscaster, and who some of you might remember from his contributions to the fore-runner of *Caribbean Magazine*, *Call in the Caribbean*. Trevor was selected from thirteen nominees, and when Ron Ramden talked to him he asked Trevor how he chooses his ties: to match his suit or his shirt.
Trevor Macdonald:	Well, I think it's probably to match, uh, shirts because, um, I'll be, I have a lot of problems if it was to match, um, suits. I have very few suits as it turns out, but thousands of shirts, so it's a very easy business selecting ties for shirts and not suits. They, they have to blend, I suppose, in, in, in some way, and occasionally I'm told that the colours don't quite go, but basically it's shirts and in that there's a very sort of simple rule I use really, is that if you like colourful ties as I tend to then you wear plain shirts.
Ron Ramden:	Does your choice of tie vary with your mood?
Trevor Macdonald:	I've never consciously thought that, but now that you say it, it is quite possible that it, it does. Some mornings you get up and it's awfully grey and cold and, um, um, and you either, you, you feel two things, either you must cheer yourself up and the general surroundings by wearing a brightly coloured tie or you succumb totally to the mood and you wear something rather dour and, um, uh, and boring. I think I probably tend to go for the brighter ones and so I think I overcome the grey surroundings or the grey weather and wear something far more interesting than outside looks.
Ron Ramden:	Do you think ties reflect the personality?
Trevor Macdonald:	I don't know, I'm, I'm told that they probably do, in which case I would find it rather difficult to define my personality by the ties I wear, because there are times when I feel that, um, I like sort of conventional ties which are striped and so on, and there are times I like ties which,

Practice Test 1

	um, are very flowery and, and look, you know, a bit flamboyant, and I suppose one, one could say that this reflects the sort of diverse personality that one has, that one is at base probably slightly conventional and one tries to pretend that one is not and that one is far more adventurous than, um, than one really is. If that's the case then my ties I suppose reflect my personality because for some occasions, on some, for long, long days I would wear fairly ordinary run-of-the-mill ties, um, and then I think well this is much too boring and, er, I go for something else. So maybe that is the kind of schizophrenia that, that one has and is demonstrated by what one wears.
Ron Ramden:	What do you think your ties say about you?
Trevor Macdonald:	Well, I think they say that perhaps there's, um, a more interesting person trying to burst out of this boring shell.

pause

tone
Now you will hear the piece again. [The piece is repeated.]

pause

That is the end of the second part of the test.

pause

Third part
You will hear an interview with Angela Blackstone, who writes books for children. Your question paper has a number of statements, numbered 18 to 24. Listen to what Angela Blackstone says, and tick the boxes to show whether the statements on the paper are true or false. You will hear the piece twice.

pause

tone

ANGELA BLACKSTONE

Presenter:	A jolly, 24-page book for small children. Nice bright pictures, but entitled 'I Have Allergies'; or another, 'I Use A Stick' or 'Skeletons and Mummies'; 'Caterpillars To Moths'; many others. Heavy subjects? Dry subjects? Well, Angela Blackstone, whose idea this series was, works from the principle that information for small children doesn't have to be dull. And obviously, for it's a very popular series, lots of children agree with her. Fiona Bodger asked Angela Blackstone what she saw as the most important function of a children's book.
Angela Blackstone:	I think the most important thing about books is that they encourage enjoyment of, of reading ... not necessarily literacy, but actually, sort of, to get people wanting to read books, because I think that all through our lives they're the one thing that let us understand how other people think, and which no other media can do as well. You know, you can, you can hear what somebody's thinking in their head in a book, or be told what somebody's thinking in their head, and no other media gives you this. So what I very much want to do is encourage children to actually love books.

Fiona Bodger: There's a very strong trend to have lavishly produced children's books which are really concentrating on fantasy, the imaginary. Do you think this is a good thing? A healthy thing?

Angela Blackstone: Well, for young children I think it's totally unnecessary. I mean the world is such an exciting, super place, and there's so much to learn about it, that I don't think they want this fantasy. I think that, you know the fantasy's perhaps trying to attract parents and grandparents and teachers to buy the books, rather than appealing to the children. But I think certainly for young children, that it's totally unnecessary.

Fiona Bodger: How do you go about getting good illustrations for your books and what kind of criteria do you adopt for, er, for finding an illustration and matching the right picture for the, for the text?.

Angela Blackstone: When I'm writing myself I do, er, I, I do brief the illustrator with the things that I want her or him to put in the illustrations because, er, particularly again, writing for young children, it is important that the illustrations are telling the same story and adding to it in different ways that you can add to it without words and also that they're very clear, because, for young children I think they get confused by sort of muddly illustrations. Again, going back to these fantasy books I think that a lot of the illustrations in them are not understood by children; they're, they're beautiful pictures, and so I do try and aim for very clear illustrations that do show exactly what's going on. For instance, if I'm, um, if I'm doing a book that's got machinery in it, er, well, I use somebody who actually understands machinery to illustrate it because I, well I certainly couldn't make a, a tractor that works, but, you know, I, well I use an engineer to do the illustrations so that the tractor does work.

Fiona Bodger: Do you in fact sort of go back to children, and talk to your own children and say 'What do you think of this?'?

Angela Blackstone: Well, I go into schools a lot and read to children and talk to children about books and so, well yes, yes, I'm getting a continuous feedback of, you know, of what they like and what they don't like and of course young children are very willing to tell you what they don't like, so, it's, you know, much more able to do so very often than adults.

Presenter: Well, I don't absolutely agree with Angela Blackstone about fantasy. It seems to me children need both fantasy and fact. But I do entirely agree with her that the informative book can be fun as these little paperbacks prove.

pause

tone

Now you will hear the piece again. [The piece is repeated.]

pause

That is the end of the third part of the test.

There will now be a pause to allow you to check your work. The question papers will then be collected by your supervisor.

pause

tone

That is the end of the test.

Practice Test 1

Paper 5: Interview (15–20 minutes)

CULTURE

The following sample package of oral examiner's material enables a complete interview to be given and assessed according to the marking scales given on pages 13 and 14.
 The photographs, passages and activities for Practice Test 1 can be found on pages 109–112 in the Student's Book.

Photographs

Ask the candidate(s) to look at these three photographs. It is Interview Exercise 1 at the back of the Student's Book.

1

Allow a suitable short interval for candidate(s) to study the photographs and then initiate discussion along these lines:

Describe/compare the people;
                  the setting;
                  the event.

Discuss different types of cultural entertainment;
         the importance of the arts;
         should artistic appreciation be 'taught' as part of education?

If a group of two or three candidates is being interviewed, encourage individuals to initiate a discussion on one topic, and invite other candidates to comment.

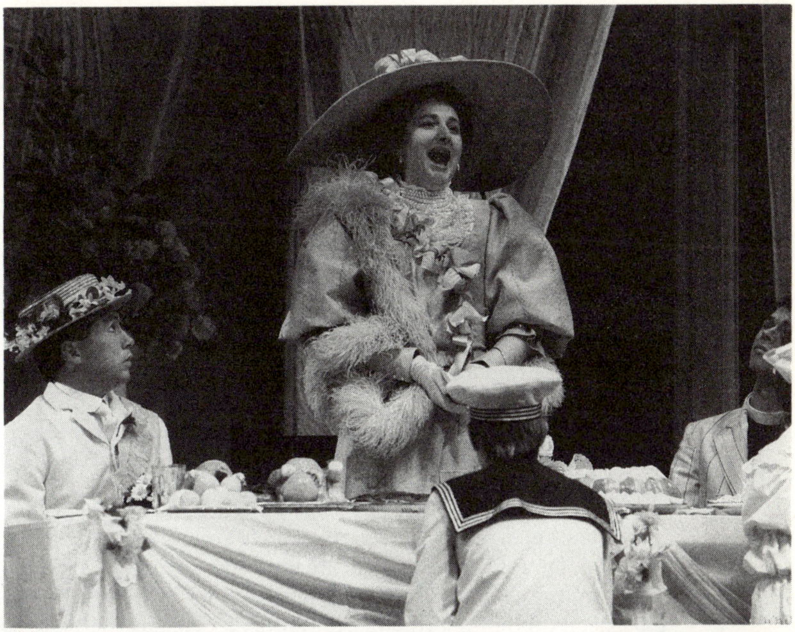

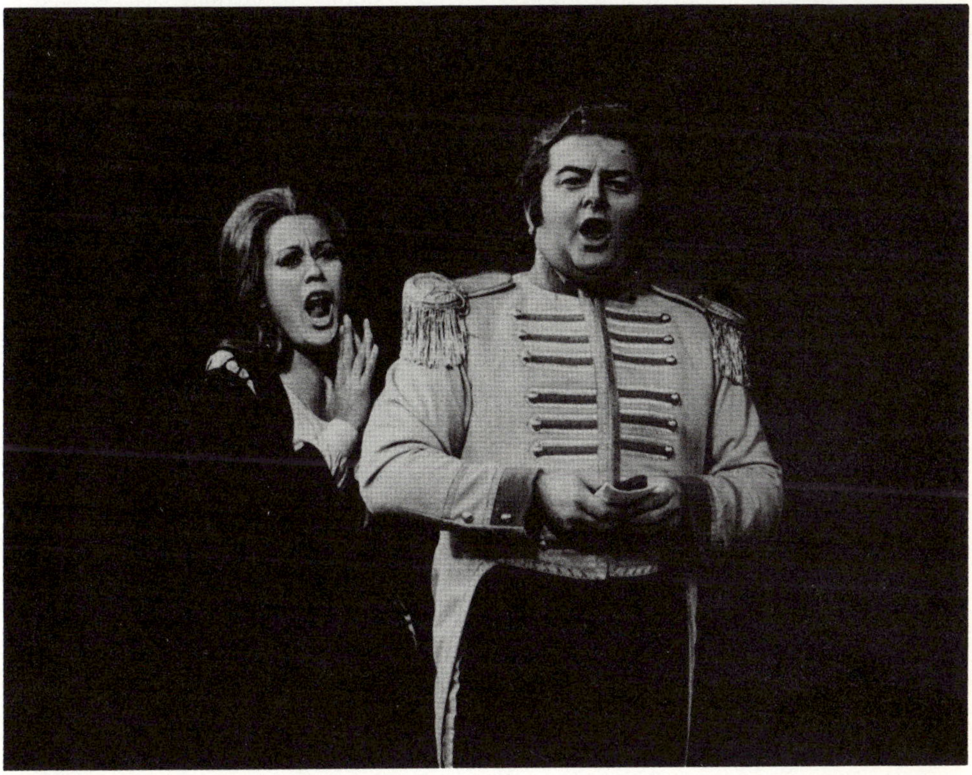

Practice Test 1

Passages

Ask the candidate(s) to look at one or more of the passages: Interview Exercises 2, 3 and 4. Invite comment on the content and possible source of the text, who the author or speaker is likely to be, and, where appropriate, what the purpose of the passage is. Comments may also include an expression of agreement or disagreement, interpretation and so on. Candidates must not be encouraged simply to read a whole passage aloud, but may quote from it where this arises naturally during the course of the discussion.

2 Taking the trouble to X-ray Manet's work may, at first, seem absurd. Why bother to probe beneath the surface of paintings which look so candid, spontaneous and decisively organised? What chance would there be of discovering dramatic changes by an artist who always appears so free of agonising doubt? As for building an entire exhibition around the results of a comprehensive X-ray examination of his key canvasses, the notion sounds frankly eccentric.

3 Both the week's other movies, *Miracles* (Cannon, Panton Street, PG) and *Jake speed* (Cannon, Haymarket, 15) are the sort of thing you only normally come across on the shelves of your local video shop. Why this particular pair should have been thought worthy of promoting in cinemas is hard to say. They are so bad that one cannot imagine how anyone of sound mind would have invested a dollar, let alone six or seven million, in either.

4 She took up drums after instantly copying percussion patterns which a woman demonstrator at a local youth centre told her had taken months to learn. She was also a star of local brass bands while a student. 'The music department was so proud of me it used to use me as an example to the boys. I don't agree with all that now – you know: "If a girl can do it, why can't you?" – but it gave me a lot of confidence at the time.'

Discussion

Ask the candidate(s) to look at the four book covers in Interview Exercise 5. Explain that 'The Pelican' is a school magazine and ask candidate(s) to decide which cover should be on the front of next month's magazine.

5

and/or

Invite the candidate(s) to read through Interview Exercise 6:

6 The examiner will ask you to imagine the following situation:

Due to a lengthy strike, or other long-term breakdown, there will be no television in your country for several months.

You will be asked to estimate the effect of this T.V. blackout
a) on your own way of life;
b) on the society you live in.

Allow a suitable period for preparation. Encourage well-developed treatment of the topic.

Practice Test 2

Paper 1: Reading Comprehension (1 hour)

Section A   One mark for each correct answer.

1 B	6 D	11 D	16 A	21 B
2 B	7 D	12 C	17 A	22 D
3 D	8 A	13 C	18 B	23 A
4 D	9 A	14 C	19 D	24 C
5 C	10 C	15 D	20 A	25 B

Section B   Two marks for each correct answer.

26 B	31 C	36 D
27 A	32 D	37 B
28 D	33 C	38 C
29 B	34 B	39 A
30 C	35 D	40 A

Total: 55

Paper 2: Composition (2 hours)

Give each composition a mark out of 20, according to the scale shown on page 4. If necessary, look at the sample compositions on pages 5–9 for further guidance on the standards required at each grade in the mark scheme.

Total: 40

Paper 3: Use of English (2 hours)

A complete mark scheme is given for each question. The 'raw' total of 79 for this paper would be adjusted to a mark out of 40 in the exam itself. Candidates passing the examination as a whole would be expected to score about 60% of the total marks.

Section A

Question 1   Give one mark for each correct answer.

1 until/till
2 not (no alternatives)
3 opposed/counter/contrary/alien
4 carried
5 been
6 such/relevant/recorded/documented/recent/particular (Other suitable adjectives may be allowed here.)

7 to/for
8 into (**not** in)
9 course
10 made/forced/brought/compelled
11 while/as/when (**not** since)
12 blocked/obscured
13 for
14 kept
15 was
16 at/over
17 under/in
18 possible/easy/simple/feasible/practicable etc.
19 what/something
20 extremely/excessively/appallingly etc. (Must begin with a vowel.)

Total: 20

Question 2

Give one mark for each word or phrase between the vertical lines. Ignore the words printed in italics.

a) *There was* | severe criticism (by many people) | *of the proposals for the new motorway.*

b) *For such* | an experienced and able teacher | discipline was not a problem. |
   | a capable teacher |

c) *Never* | before had a/any/the King resigned. |

d) *The identity* | of the murdered man was given/notified/revealed/made known (to the police). |

e) *It is a mystery* | (as to) what (has) happened to | *the two climbers.*

f) *Swearing at the referee earned* | him two match suspensions.
   | him a two-match suspension.
   | (him) a suspension (for him) for two matches. |

g) *In spite of* | his innocence | *he was executed.*
   | his/him not being guilty
   | not being guilty
   | the fact that he was innocent/not guilty |

h) *Nobody who* | has not / hasn't ever / has never been/ travelled abroad should
   | has (always) stayed/remained in his/her/their home/native/own country should | *criticise foreign customs.*

Total: 9

Question 3

Give one mark for each word or phrase between the vertical lines. Ignore the words printed in italics.

a) *That cheese is mouldy;* | I wouldn't/shouldn't touch/eat it if
   | I would throw/chuck it away/out if
   | I would send it / take it back / complain about it if | *I were you.*

Practice Test 2

b) *As long as it leads to a good career* | it makes no difference
it doesn't matter
it is of no interest/consequence |
to me what course of study you follow.

c) *You had a lucky escape. You* | could've/might've been
were (very) nearly | *killed.*

d) *You'll have to* | get rid
dispose | *of that old dustbin. There's a hole in it.*

e) *In order to get better results* | try
you could start by
you should think about
you should consider | *adding a little more flour.*

f) *'You should go and look for a job, not sit around doing nothing.'*
'Why don't you mind | your own business?' |

Total: 6

Question 4

Give one mark for each word or phrase between the vertical lines. Ignore the words printed in italics.

a) *The Head Teacher* | was at a loss | *to comprehend/understand the girl's behaviour.*

b) | Your nephew will be suspected of stealing/having stolen | *the money.*

c) | No matter how hard Fred tried (to start the car) | (any correct ending) |

d) | The Arnolds look on/upon Henry | as a | *good friend.*

e) | Only Jane succeeded
| No one but Jane succeeded | in producing | *the correct answer.*

f) The new ambassador has (a) wide knowledge of | *current affairs.*
The new ambassador's knowledge of | *current affairs* | is very wide. (1 mark)

g) | Theirs was a/the | *conventional, middle-class* | upbringing. |

h) | United are/is bound to beat City.
| City are/is bound to be beaten by United. |

Total: 12

Practice Test 2

Section B

Question 5

Give the mark shown for each question for coherent and relevant answers, not necessarily echoing the wording given here.

a) When cornered/trapped/they can't escape.   1
b) To fight when rivalry/fear is the main factor / driving force (1) rather than the need to obtain food (1).   2
c) Lion lacks aggression/hostility / feels hungry.   1
d) When animals offer resistance/fear retaliation / when opponents fight back. (Gloss essential.)   1
e) An attack by a defending force against an attacking enemy / fighting or attacking back.   1
f) (Any definition which relies on idea of overwhelming/thronging/surrounding one's enemy (1) idea of group/crowd/large numbers (1).)   2
g) Drives off enemy (enables attacked to survive) (1) interrupts/spoils hunting for predator (1).   2
h) Teaching young/inexperienced birds how to recognise/be aware of an enemy.   1
i) Educational.   1
j) Making life difficult for one's enemy (any appropriate gloss).   1
k) Jackdaws use active/physical attacking tactics (1) geese don't actually attack (i.e. no physical attack) (1).   2
l) Does not want to give an impression of fear/being frightened/submission/being dominated/losing/defeated etc., (**not** losing face). (Gloss essential.)   1
m) When animals are in a herd / en masse / in large numbers.   1
n) Instinctive/inherited/ingrained response/reaction in domestic animals.   1
o) Writer jumped into lake when threatened by cattle (1) brother climbed up a tree when threatened by pigs (1).   2
p) Award 5 marks for ability to extract relevant *information*, giving 1 mark for reference to each animal and method, i.e.:

     wagtails, birds – spoil hunting / drive other birds from hunting ground (survival factor common to all) (1)
     jackdaws – teach/train young to recognise enemy (1)
     geese and ducks – learn that certain shape/colour is dangerous in order to recognise enemies (1)
     zebras – molest (in order to survive/drive away) (1)
     cattle and pigs – encircle (ditto). (1)   5

Award up to 7 marks for ability to *summarise* effectively, in a well-written paragraph which shows the candidate has given some thought to:
     – overall construction (not mere lists)
     – use of connectors
     – economical style appropriate to a summary
     – some indication of own vocabulary (little reliance on 'lifting').   7

Total: 32

Practice Test 2

Paper 4: Listening Comprehension (about 30 minutes)

First part: Fats Domino

		Score
1	20	1
2	twice/2	1
3	1957	1
4	No	$\frac{1}{2}$
5	Yes	1
6	4	$\frac{1}{2}$
7	4	$\frac{1}{2}$
8	4	$\frac{1}{2}$

Total: 6 marks

Second part: Dinosaur

		Score
9	F	$\frac{1}{2}$
10	T	$\frac{1}{2}$
11	T	$\frac{1}{2}$
12	F	$\frac{1}{2}$
13	F	$\frac{1}{2}$
14	T	$\frac{1}{2}$
15	T	$\frac{1}{2}$
16	F	$\frac{1}{2}$
17	T	$\frac{1}{2}$
18	F	$\frac{1}{2}$

Total: 5 marks

Third part: Edinburgh

		Score
19	12, 26	½
	31, 86	½
20	7 p.m.	½
21	(the) twelfth century/C12	½
22	554 44 94	½
23	St Andrew's Square	½
24	Edinburgh Castle	½
25	1850	½
26	Scottish gifts,	½
	books and records	½
27	the King's Theatre	½
28	226 6591	½

Total: 6 marks

Transcript

This is the Certificate of Proficiency Listening Comprehension Test.
Test Number 2
You will be given a question paper for the Certificate of Proficiency Test 2. Your supervisor will give you further instructions. On the question paper you will see spaces for your name and index number, and questions for each part of the test. Each part of the test will be heard twice. There will be pauses to allow you to look through the questions before each part, and other pauses to let you think about your answers. At the end of every pause you will hear this sound.

tone

The tape will now be stopped while question papers are given out. You must ask any questions now, as you will not be allowed to speak during the test.

pause

First part
You will hear a talk about the jazz musician Fats Domino. For questions 1 to 8 fill in the missing information in the spaces provided. Only brief answers are required. You will hear the piece twice.

pause

tone

FATS DOMINO

He's one of the giants of rock and roll, but he's more than that: he's a jazzman, a blues singer, a boogie pianist and composer and he's still pulling in the audiences although he cut his first record when he was 20. He's Fats Domino. Fats is unique but you can still see the influences on his music. People like Amos Milways, Big Joe Turner, the piano player Pete Johnson and all the great boogie players, and of course Louis Armstrong. He met Armstrong twice in California and liked the way he sang 'Blueberry Hill', a song Fats himself recorded

Practice Test 2

much later, in 1957. That recording is so well known that many people think 'Blueberry Hill' is one of Fats Domino's compositions, but it isn't.

   Apart from 'Blueberry Hill', songs like 'I'm Walking' and 'I'm Going to Walk Alone', sold 2 or 3 million copies and Fats goes on recording and appearing in cabaret, which doesn't give him a lot of time with his wife and large family, four boys and four girls. Two of the boys play the piano and his youngest son, who has just left high school, goes to college this year. The girls have left college and two of them play the piano in New Orleans. Fats is in London right now. To celebrate his arrival, here's one of his favourites, 'Blue Monday'.

pause

tone
Now you will hear the piece again. [The piece is repeated.]

pause

That is the end of the first part of the test.

pause

Second part
You will now hear a discussion about dinosaurs. For each of the questions 9 to 18 tick one box to show whether the statement is true or false. You will hear the piece twice.

pause

tone

THE DISCOVERY OF A DINOSAUR BONE

Presenter: Many years ago, about one hundred and twenty-five million to be as precise as I can, a huge dinosaur was roaming through the forests of what's now become the county of Surrey, to the south of London. Nothing very odd about that. We've known that these prehistoric creatures were here from the fossilised remains that have already been found. But this one was different. Not a herbivore like all the others. This one was a flesh-eater. No doubt with a healthy appetite for its fellow dinosaurs. The existence of what until now has been a completely unknown type in Britain came with the discovery of a very large claw-bone. Today it's on display along with other parts of this vast creature at the Natural History Museum in London. According to the museum it represents one of the most exciting finds in Britain this century, and for that we have to thank an amateur fossil-collector called Bill Waller. He's been telling John Lomax about a very wet and miserable day last January when he was working in a clay-pit.

Bill Waller: Well, it was a rainy day and I hadn't been in the pit more than ten minutes and soon I just happened to walk onto some bone fragments and a smaller claw which was in two pieces but joined together nicely and then, then I found this rock nodule. I suppose it was about the size of a pineapple and I could see what looked like a piece of bone sticking out of it and I cracked it with my hammer and the whole thing fell into lots of pieces and then I, I sort of carefully collected them together, put them in a bag, brought them home,

	cleaned them up and then it began to really dawn on me what it was. To be honest, I could have cried when I whacked it and saw what came out.
John Lomax:	Once you'd stuck the bits back together, er, what did you do with it?
Bill Waller:	Well, to be completely honest, I put it on a glass shelf with some other fossils. Must have been there for three weeks at least, perhaps a month, and then my son-in-law, who is more interested in sharks' teeth, on the fossil side, was going to a museum to do some research work on his sharks' teeth and just casually said, 'Would you like me to take it in to see if I can get it identified?' and they asked if they could borrow it to take a fibre-glass copy or whether I would like to donate it to the National Collection.
John Lomax:	Didn't you feel at any time any sort of proprietorial concern over it? Didn't you really feel that this was your special find and you wanted to keep it.
Bill Waller:	No, I was, I was very pleased to have a nice claw, obviously, but no, no, I hadn't attached that amount of importance to it myself. To me, it was just a nice fossil.
John Lomax:	But it turns out to be the kind of fossil that most professionals would give their right arm to have found.
Bill Waller:	Oh yes, there's no doubt about that, thinking about it. But this is fossil-hunting. You never know what you are going to find. It's pot-luck. I just happened to be the lucky guy who walked on to it.
John Lomax:	Now the experts have had a chance to look at the bone, what kind of dinosaur are we talking about here? What kind of, eh, description are they giving?
Bill Waller:	Well, I think the claw proper makes it clear that it was carnivorous, and there's not too many of those found in Britain, apparently.
John Lomax:	Well, it looks as though it's a completely new species. If that's the case it's going to need a new name. Are you hoping that it may end up being called Tyrannosaurus Bill Waller.
Bill Waller:	Huh, yeah, well, I think that's just wishful thinking.

pause

tone

Now you will hear the piece again. [The piece is repeated.]

pause

That is the end of the second part of the test.

pause

Third part
You will hear a recorded telephone announcement giving details about visiting Edinburgh, in Scotland. For questions 19 to 28 fill in the missing information in the spaces provided. You will hear the piece twice.

pause

tone

EDINBURGH LEISURE LINE SERVICE: SATURDAY 6th AUGUST

Welcome to Edinburgh. We have some suggestions for ways in which you might like to spend your day in and around the capital.

Practice Test 2

Edinburgh Zoo has Scotland's finest collection of wild animals and is open between 9a.m. and 6p.m., 365 days a year. The largest colony of penguins in any zoo shares a beautiful parkland setting that includes over 300 different species. Bring the family and spend the day at the zoo. It's only 15 minutes from the city centre. Buses to and from the zoo are numbers 12, 26, 31 and 86. Car parking facilities are also available.

Your entertainment at the Ross Open Air Theatre in Princes Street Gardens begins today at 3p.m. with a concert given by the Regimental Band of The Queen's Own Hussars. From 7p.m. John Wilson and his Band provide the music for the Old Time Dance Championships, 'Come Dancing'.

The historical Duddingston Kirk beside Duddingston Loch is open to visitors today. Teas will be served in this twelfth-century church in the afternoon. It will be open from 10a.m. until 6p.m. today.

One of the best ways to see this beautiful and historic city is by joining one of the many coach tours organised by Lothian Regional Transport. These tours cover all parts of the city and leave from Waverley Bridge, just off Princes Street, throughout the day. For details, please phone 554 4494.

Most of Scotland is on Edinburgh's doorstep. You will be surprised just how much you can see of it in one day. Scottish Omnibus operate an extensive and varied programme of day and afternoon tours every day from St Andrew's Square. Phone 556 8464.

If the weather is clear, why not visit the Wellhouse Tower and Camera Obscura at the top of the Royal Mile near Edinburgh Castle. Here you can look out on magnificent views of Edinburgh and beyond through this unique optical device installed in 1850. There is also a Scottish gift, book and record shop. The Camera Obscura is open every day between 9.30a.m. and 5p.m.

For your entertainment in the theatre this evening, the King's Theatre in Leven Street presents Peter Morrison and his guests, who introduce the audience to the fine Scottish tradition of popular singing. This show begins at 8p.m.

To find out more about events or places to visit, please call at the Tourist Information Centre at 5 Waverley Bridge, or telephone 226 6591.

We do hope you enjoy your day in the capital and thank you for calling.

pause

tone
Now you will hear the piece again. [The piece is repeated.]

pause

That is the end of the third part of the test.

There will now be a pause to allow you to check your work. The question papers will then be collected by your supervisor.

pause

tone
That is the end of the test.

Practice Test 2

Paper 5: Interview (15–20 minutes)

ADVERTISING

The following sample package of oral examiner's material enables a complete interview to be given and assessed according to the marking scales given on pages 13 and 14.

The photographs, passages and activities for Practice Test 2 can be found on pages 112–116 in the Student's Book.

Photographs

Ask the candidate(s) to look at the photographs below and on page 40. It is Interview Exercise 7 at the back of the Student's Book.

7

Allow a suitable short interval for candidate(s) to study the photographs and then initiate discussion along these lines:

Describe/compare the setting:
         the people;
         the atmosphere.
Discuss the effectiveness of advertisements in public places;
        whether outdoor advertising spoils the urban scene;
        advertising and sponsorship in sport;
        whether sportsmen/women should advertise cigarettes or alcohol.

If a group of two or three candidates is being interviewed, encourage individuals to initiate a discussion on one topic, and invite other candidates to comment.

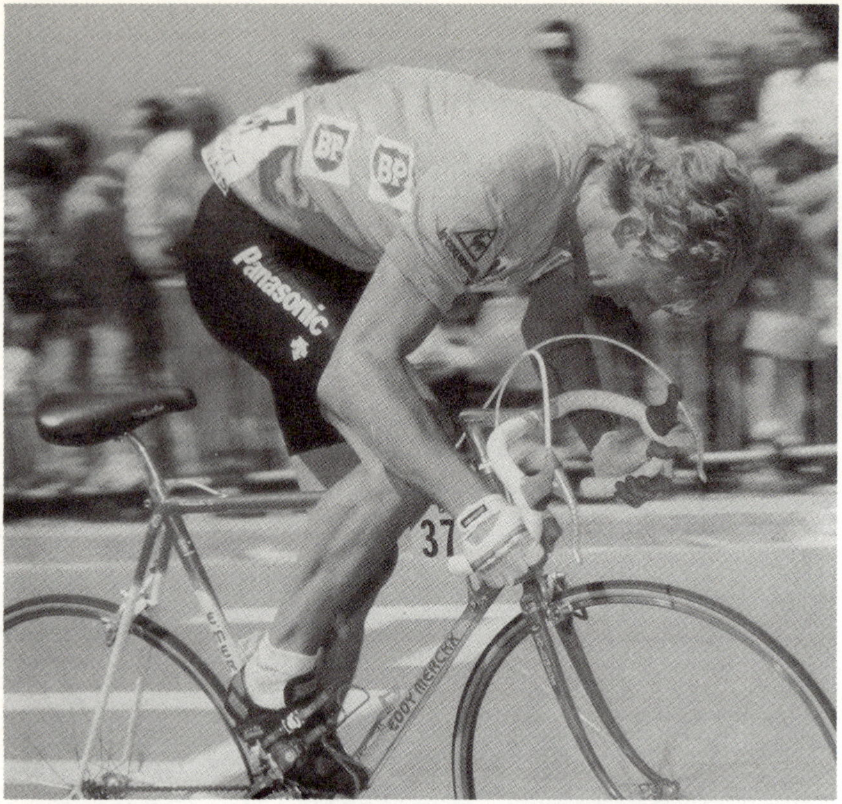
BP
BP
Panasonic
37
EDDY MERCKX

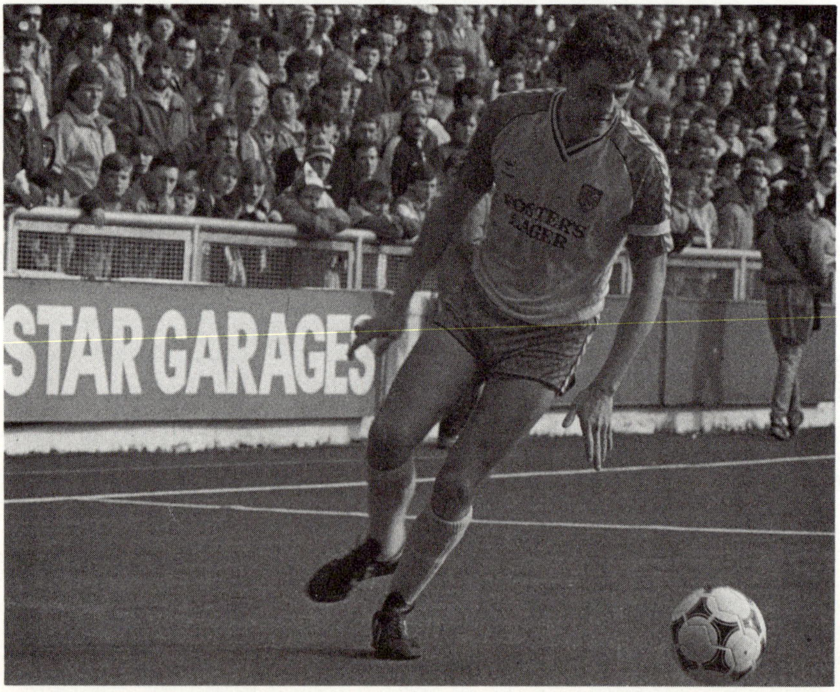
STAR GARAGES
LAGER

Passages

Ask the candidate(s) to look at one or more of the passages: Interview Exercises 8, 9 and 10. Invite comment on the content and possible source of the text, who the author or speaker is likely to be, and, where appropriate, what the purpose of the passage is. Comments may also include an expression of agreement or disagreement, interpretation and so on. Candidates must not be encouraged simply to read a whole passage aloud, but may quote from it where this arises naturally during the course of the discussion.

8 Considerations of how the nature of the product or service will influence the nature of the message.
   Can it be treated humorously or seriously? Should the emphasis be on lengthy, technical explanation of the product in operation? Is visual treatment important? Is the product or service best portrayed in an atmosphere of escapism or romance? What is known about why users buy this category of product or service and how will this influence the nature of the message?

9 Supermom stayed home and when the kiddies came back from school she baked them cookies in the shape of pumpkins with raisin eyes and carrot noses. But now we have before us the ideal of Superwoman, who prepares a well-balanced nutritious breakfast for her children, and her children eat it. She goes off to work where she makes $30,000 a year as an executive of a law firm. She comes home and reads to the children, then serves dinner by candlelight to her husband.

10 Nature has the answer for blocked-up stuffy noses. Natural Olbas Oil. Just a few drops of natural Olbas Oil on a tissue or handkerchief, and a deep breathe-in gives immediate relief. For catarrh, colds, sinus and nasal congestion.
   Olbas Oil is the unique blend of 6 natural pure plant oils and menthol Cajuput, cloves, eucalyptus, peppermint, wintergreen, and juniper berries. For all the family, including the children.

Discussion

Ask the candidate(s) to look at the advertisements for language courses in Interview Exercise 11. Invite the candidate(s) to study the bold type and main features of each, and say:

– Which advertisement has most impact and why.
– What advertising techniques are used.
– How effective they are.
– How honest they are.

Practice Test 2

11 Learn to speak a new language. Anytime! Anywhere!

Speak French, German or Spanish with ease in 30-45 hours – *or all your money back!*

How would you like to speak another language? Of course you would. Haven't the time? If you've time to drive a car ... or have a bath, you've time to learn a second language. How? With the Language Courses from Reader's Digest. Just pop on a cassette whenever you have some spare moments, then listen and repeat. You have no boring textbooks to read ... no complicated grammar to learn. Think how much time you waste in traffic jams. You could be using that time to learn another language.

So don't waste any more time: fill in the coupon and send for your free cassette and brochure right away.

Learn in your spare moments

FREE ◄◄ DEMONSTRATION CASSETTE

Send now for your demonstration cassette and start learning right away. There's absolutely no obligation.

Reader's Digest

SPEAK FRENCH IN ONLY 3 MONTHS! (or German, Spanish, Italian, Dutch, Swedish, Portuguese or Greek)

Radio Times readers now have an opportunity to buy the world-famous Hugo Cassette Course for **ONLY £25.95** – a saving of £5.00 on the normal price – **plus a free pocket dictionary.**

At this special price it is an unbeatable investment for business or pleasure, for yourself, your company, or your family. You could pay a lot more for a language course of such high quality. With Hugo there is no risk; you may listen to the course for two weeks at home and return it for a full refund of your money if you are not absolutely satisfied.

*SPECIAL OFFER £5 SAVING!
AND
FREE! WITH EVERY ORDER...
POCKET DICTIONARY
(This offer closes on 16.3.87)

WHICH OF THESE LANGUAGES WOULD YOU LIKE TO SPEAK?

☐ Afrikaans
☐ American English
☐ Arabic (Modern)
☐ Chinese (Mandarin)
☐ Danish
☐ Dutch
☐ English
☐ Finnish
☐ French
☐ German
☐ Greek (Modern)
☐ Hebrew (Modern)
☐ Hindi
☐ Icelandic
☐ Indonesian
☐ Irish
☐ Italian
☐ Japanese
☐ Korean
☐ Malay
☐ Norwegian
☐ Polish
☐ Portuguese
☐ Russian
☐ Serbo-Croat
☐ Spanish (Castilian)
☐ Spanish (Latin American)
☐ Swedish
☐ Thai
☐ Welsh

Tick the one you want to speak in 3 months' time...

It's really a lot easier and faster than you'd expect when you learn the Linguaphone way. You simply learn at your own pace, as and when it suits you best. And you'll be following a course prepared by some of the world's leading language experts. You'll get the accent right, too. With Linguaphone, all it takes is as little as half an hour a day and you could be speaking a new language in 3 months from now.

For your FREE **DEMONSTRATION PACK** containing cassette, course booklet and full-colour brochure, simply complete and post the coupon now.

FREE OFFER

Free! This personal stereo cassette player is yours free when you order your Linguaphone language course.

and/or

Role-play

Invite the candidate(s) to imagine that they are part of an advertising team working to promote a new kind of soft drink. Ask them to discuss and decide how and where they should market their new product to achieve the best results, considering the guidelines given below.

12 *Advertising guidelines*
- What market are we aiming at?
- What kind of image do we want to project?
- What type of attitude shall we adopt – amusing, serious, sexy, scientific etc.?
- What will be the most effective places to advertise our product – television, magazines, newspapers, cinema, street posters etc.?

Practice Test 3

Paper 1: Reading Comprehension (1 hour)

Section A One mark for each correct answer.

1 A	6 C	11 A	16 B	21 C
2 A	7 B	12 C	17 C	22 C
3 D	8 C	13 C	18 B	23 A
4 C	9 C	14 B	19 D	24 D
5 B	10 C	15 C	20 A	25 A

Section B Two marks for each correct answer.

26 C	31 C	36 C
27 B	32 A	37 A
28 C	33 D	38 B
29 B	34 B	39 C
30 C	35 C	40 C

Total: 55

Paper 2: Composition (2 hours)

Give each composition a mark out of 20, according to the scale shown on page 4. If necessary, look at the sample compositions on pages 5–9 for further guidance on the standards required at each grade in the mark scheme.

Total: 40

Practice Test 3

Paper 3: Use of English (2 hours)

A complete mark scheme is given for each question. The 'raw' total of 75 for this paper would be adjusted to a mark out of 40 in the exam itself. Candidates passing the examination as a whole would be expected to score about 60% of the total marks.

Section A

Question 1   Give one mark for each correct answer.

1 This/That
2 making
3 never
4 are
5 In
6 down
7 fire
8 be
9 nothing/little
10 fact
11 so
12 will
13 even
14 it/through
15 up
16 into/through/to
17 causing
18 ignore/neglect
19 now
20 done/undertaken

Total: 20

Question 2

Give one mark for each word or phrase between the vertical lines. Ignore the words printed in italics.

a) *Only by* | united opposition | can/will/could we eliminate world terrorism. |
   | can/will/could world terrorism be eliminated. |

b) *If it hadn't* | been for her (insistence/insisting on) kissing | *everyone goodbye she would have caught the train*.

c) *Throughout* | his life the fisherman was very poor / suffered from great poverty. |

d) *It* | has been suggested that | income tax (should) be abolished. |
   | we/they/the government etc. should abolish income tax. |

e) *Cooking* | (for five hungry children) is no fun / gives me no pleasure. |

f) *No matter* | what I do | my parents find fault with it/me. |

g) *I have* | no intention of replying to | *that rude letter from Edward*.

h) *The operation left* | Simon feeling | weaker than he (had) expected. |

Total: 12

Question 3

Give one mark for each word or phrase between the vertical lines. Ignore the words printed in italics.

a) *In spite of* | being/feeling | *unwell the Prime Minister continued her tour of the factory*.

b) *Helen's away this week, so it's* | useless/pointless/a waste of time/senseless (trying) to (try and) | *ring her*.

45

Practice Test 3

c) *Should you ever be* | in need | *of assistance, contact this number.*

d) *I am* | having/going to have the (any reasonable suggestion) | *painted pink to match the carpet and curtains*.

e) *Frescobaldi's theory about perpetual motion was fascinating, but it was impossible* | to put (it) into | *practice*.

f) *The party was great: you really* | should/ought to have | *come*.

Total: 6

Question 4

Give one mark for each word or phrase between the vertical lines. Ignore the words printed in italics.

a) | There has been a steady decline | in the rate of inflation | *during recent months*.

b) | (It was) Derek (who) drew my attention to the mistake. |

c) | They were about/ready/going/preparing to | call off the match | *when the opposition arrived*.

d) | The concert was poorly attended. |

e) | The train was due to leave five minutes ago. |

f) | The expiry date on/of/for this licence is | *December 31st 1987*.

g) | There is little/not much/nothing to choose between these/the two essays. |

h) | Most doctors agree that smoking does/can/will harm you/your health. |

Total: 10

Section B

Question 5

Give the mark shown for each question for coherent and relevant answers, not necessarily echoing the wording given here.

a) No aptitude for/interest in (1) sports/games etc. (explanation of 'athletic' required) (1).   2

b) (Any idea of falseness/incorrectness/simpleness, lack of thought.)   1

c) Athletes/sportsmen.   1

d) (Idea of praise/admiration (1) for (qualities that are) insignificant/unimportant/unreal (1).)   2

e) Personal skills / qualities for adult life / what has been learned at school / knowledge (**not** just athletic expertise).   1

f) They do not value it as highly as sporting ability (comparison essential).   1

g) (Clear expression of (human) values/ideals (1) which are those of wild beasts (1) if we

	value sporting ability too highly (1).)	3
h)	(Idea of sport as an object of worship (1) encouraging the finest human values (1).)	2
i)	(The religion of) sport.	1
j)	People who believe in fair play, honesty etc. (1)	1
k)	A way/method/means by which people can demonstrate (1) their essential character – good or bad (1).	2
l)	Ten marks as follows: Excessive hero-worship is bad for the athlete (1). Excessive concentration on sport neglects necessary adult life skills (1). Over-emphasis on athleticism under-values academic ability (1). Excessive value attached to sport leads to jungle values (1). Worship of sport is unjustified as sport does not create excellence of character (1). Plus: A clear expression of the writer's attitudes to these beliefs (1). Up to 4 marks for the candidate's ability to demonstrate good summarising skills, proper expression, connected paragraph construction (4). (Answers that are long, rambling, unconnected and make excessive use of lifting should score nil.)	5 1 4

Total: 27

Paper 4: Listening Comprehension (about 30 minutes)

First part: Arts Club enquiry

		Score
1	Thursday	½
2	once a month	½
3	Park Avenue	½
4	Friday evenings/every Friday evening	½
5	not given	½
6	£2.50 (each)	½
7	Appleton Arts Club	½
8	(a) newsletter	½
9	Players	½
10	Gramophone Circle Music Workshop	½

Total: 5½ marks

Practice Test 3

Second part: Polio tricycles

		Score
11	F	½
12	T	½
13	T	½
14	F	½
15	F	½
16	T	½
17	F	½
18	F	½
19	T	½

Total: 4½ marks

Third part: Holiday plans

		Score
20	C	1
21	C	1
22	B	1
23	C	1
24	A	1

Total: 5 marks

Fourth part: A translator

		Score
25	B	1
26	C	1
27	D	1
28	A	1
29	A	1

Total: 5 marks

Transcript

This is the Certificate of Proficiency Listening Comprehension Test.
Test Number 3
You will be given a question paper for the Certificate of Proficiency Test 3. Your supervisor will give you further instructions. On the question paper you will see spaces for your name and index number, and questions for each part of the test. Each part of the test will be heard twice. There will be pauses to allow you to look through the questions before each part, and other pauses to let you think about your answers. At the end of every pause you will hear this sound.

tone

Practice Test 3

The tape will now be stopped while question papers are given out. You must ask any questions now, as you will not be allowed to speak during the test.

pause

First part
You will hear a telephone conversation between Mr Harding and Frances Drew about joining a club. For questions 1 to 10 fill in the missing information in the spaces provided. You will hear the piece twice.

pause

tone

ARTS CLUB ENQUIRY

Mr Harding: Hello.
Frances: Hello. Is that Appleton 363?
Mr Harding: It is, Harding speaking.
Frances: Oh, um, are you, I mean, I'd like to speak to the Secretary of the Arts Club.
Mr Harding: Yes, speaking.
Frances: Oh, oh, hello. My name is Frances Drew. I've just moved to the area, my husband and I, and we'd be interested in joining the Arts Club, but we'd like some more information really, you know, about joining and the sort of activities you do.
Mr Harding: Yes well, what you want's our calendar. Ask at the library. I'll make sure there are plenty there by say Thursday. That alright for you?
Frances: Yes, fine thank you. But, erm, would you mind telling me how much it costs to join?
Mr Harding: Membership fee – for an adult it's two pounds fifty, per annum of course.
Frances: What exactly does club membership entitle one to?
Mr Harding: Entitle you to? Ooh, for a start there's the, er, club events – you get invited to them of course. They're for members only and, eh, they are free . . .
Frances: What sort of events are they, I mean . . . ?
Mr Harding: You'll see what they are when you get hold of a calendar. But, well, there's the club evenings for instance, once a month, usually Wednesdays from 8 till about 10.
Frances: And whereabouts do you hold them?
Mr Harding: Club evenings? The Beach Pavillion, do you know it?
Frances: No, I don't think I do. It's not near the seafront is it?
Mr Harding: No, up past the tennis courts on Park Avenue, you know where that is?
Frances: No, I'm afraid I don't. We'd soon find it in the car though.
Mr Harding: Quite. I don't know what your interests are – music, got any musical talents?
Frances: I'm not sure about talents exactly. I like music – we both do.
Mr Harding: Do either of you sing?
Frances: Oh, yes, we've both been in choirs.
Mr Harding: There you are then, the club's got a very fine choir, very fine. I'm in it myself as a matter of fact. We have practices every Friday evening . . . and it's no good just thinking of joining if you can't make the practices.
Frances: No of course not, but what's the procedure, I mean if we decide to join the choir, or any of the other activities, how do we go about it?

49

Practice Test 3

Mr Harding: You can't get in the choir without an audition. As far as the other sections are concerned, members have to apply through the Section Secretary in the first place.
Frances: Yes right. And the fee again – I've written it down somewhere.
Mr Harding: £2.50 each.
Frances: And where do we send it, to you?
Mr Harding: No, I'm the Secretary. It's the Treasurer who deals with that. I'll give you his name if you want to write it down.
Frances: Yes, please.
Mr Harding: His name's Hosegood, H-O-S-E and then good.
Frances: Yes.
Mr Harding: Initial P. Address . . . 3 Clayhills, Appleton.
Frances: Right, and it's alright to send a cheque?
Mr Harding: That's the usual, yes. Payable to Appleton Arts Club. Oh, and, er, better put your address on the back as you're new. Oh, and incidently there's a newsletter out three times a year, just to keep club members up to date with what's going on; they, they're sent out to everyone.
Frances: That's good. Um, just one last thing. Would you mind telling me what the other sections are just so that I can tell my husband and we . . .
Mr Harding: The Players – that's our acting group I've told you. Choir you know about. There's the Gramophone Circle, the Music Workshop, the Literary and Discussion Group – oh, that one meets in different members' homes. Then there's the Studio Workshop, and, er, what have I missed out? Oh, yes the Arts Talks, that's the lot I think . . . ah, the Film Society, that's the other one. Got them all?
Frances: Um, yes, just about. Thank you very much – you've been very helpful.
Mr Harding: Not at all, pleased to assist, and, eh, look forward to meeting you and your husband at the club.
Frances: Yes, thank you. Goodbye then.

pause

tone
Now you will hear the piece again. [*The piece is repeated.*]

pause

That is the end of the first part of the test.

pause

Second part
You will hear part of a radio programme in which aids to help handicapped children are discussed. For questions 11 to 19 tick one box to show whether the statement is true or false. You will hear the piece twice.

pause

tone

POLIO TRICYCLES

Presenter: Kennet Westmacott is the director of a unit that does research into aids to help handicapped children and one thing that he's been interested

	in is polio tricycles for children who've lost the use of their legs. So the pedals are on the handlebars, if you can imagine it, and you work them by hand to drive the front wheel. Recently Kennet was working in the city of Blantyre, which is in Malawi, when, as he told Ian Williams, he heard of a young boy called Pafupi, who lived in a very remote village, and was said to have made his own polio tricycle.
Kennet Westmacott:	It had taken him approximately three years to make and he had scrounged, begged and borrowed bits of a bicycle. And so he'd really used material from bicycles that had been thrown out, so they were really, eh, beyond repair. But, er, by using a stone and a old axe blade and bits and pieces he had fashioned together with bits of wire and string and bits and pieces a, em, polio tricycle for himself.
Ian Williams:	And he'd done this by himself with no outside assistance at all?
Kennet Westmacott:	He had been operated on, um, at some time, though we couldn't find his original records. And he, he'd probably spotted a polio tricycle while he was in Blantyre undergoing the operations. You know . . . so he'd probably seen it and then just out of memory he'd made something up.
Ian Williams:	So how did it differ essentially from an ordinary tricycle?
Kennet Westmacott:	Well, for a start he'd made it so that he would travel down the ordinary bush track, which is approximately 18 inches wide, so it's a very narrow bicycle. And that was, er, one thing which was very good about it. The other thing that he had done was made it so that the bicycle could reverse.
Ian Williams:	So having found him and found the way he built this, was he able then to help you in, in your making of various aids?
Kennet Westmacott:	Well, what we did immediately after we'd found him, in fact we took the bicycle off him and we took it back to Blantyre and made him an exact copy so that he could be mobile again. And then we sat down round the drawing board and we came up with two ideas in fact, two variations on it – one that he tried and said was, er, rubbish and the other which he tried and he liked greatly. And that's the one I've actually done some drawings of.
Presenter:	And they are in fact called now Pafupi tricycles. I have a sheet of paper here in front of me from a technical publication and it is all about the Pafupi tricycle and it also has a diagrammatic drawing of it so that anybody who wanted to would be able to build one themselves. If you would like details you know where to write to, don't you?

pause

tone
Now you will hear the piece again. [The piece is repeated.]

pause

That is the end of the second part of the test.

pause

Practice Test 3

Third part
You will hear a man and a woman discussing their holiday plans. For questions 20 to 24 tick one of the boxes A, B, C or D to show the correct answer. You will hear the piece twice.

pause

tone

HOLIDAY PLANS

Man: Would you like a cup of coffee or are you still busy with the money?
Woman: I'm still going through the accounts. We've overspent dreadfully this month.
Man: By how much?
Woman: I don't know. It looks to me as if it's getting on for almost £500.
Man: Oh, does that mean we won't be able to get our holiday – have we got enough for our holiday still?
Woman: Well I'm not sure. I honestly don't think that we could afford to go really.
Man: But we haven't had a holiday for three years!
Woman: That's not the point is it, we haven't had a holiday for three years because we can't afford it and I don't think we can afford it this year. We could maybe manage a week somewhere in this country.
Man: I was really looking forward to this holiday ... three weeks in Barbados at Christmas – warmth, sea, sunshine, we haven't be ...
Woman: I know. So was I.
Man: We really need to just get away out of this country because we haven't been away for three years.
Woman: Well ... look it's just not on. I mean, we could think about somewhere ...
Man: Can't we ask your mother for the money? Can't we borrow the money from somwhere for the holiday?
Woman: Well, you know what I feel about borrowing. We're still in debt over the car. We've always said we wouldn't borrow money for things that weren't absolutely essential; a holiday isn't essential.
Man: I really feel it is this time.
Woman: Well, let's look at cheaper holidays then. Let's look at somewhere closer to home, right. Let's look at Europe.
Man: Well that's ... there's no point in going to Europe at Christmas, is there?
Woman: Well, you said you wanted to get away (*It's cold.*) from here. Well, what are you saying; that you only want to go where it is hot and sunny?
Man: Yes, I want some warmth.
Woman: Well, we can't afford it.
Man: Well I think we ought to borrow the money. Your mother would be very pleased to lend us the money.
Woman: I know she would lend it to us but that's not the point.
Man: I don't want to talk about it anymore. Let's discuss it some other time.

pause

tone
Now you will hear the piece again. [*The piece is repeated.*]

pause

That is the end of the third part of the test.

Practice Test 3

Fourth part
You will hear Lily talking about her work as a translator. For questions 25 to 29 tick one of the boxes A, B, C or D to show the correct answer. You will hear the piece twice.

pause

tone

A TRANSLATOR

Friend: What about books, do you ever do books?
Lily: Well, I was asked recently if I'd like to do a travel book. There were four countries – I had a choice of Italy, Greece, China and Japan and I wanted to do the Italian one, 'cause I probably know more about that than the other countries, but somebody else had already chosen it. So if I do do it, I should think I'll be doing the Greek one, but again, deadlines, ah, they're being a nuisance, because they want it done in less than four months and it's a very long book, and it may mean that several translators will have to work on the book – which may present difficulties if we all use different words for the same term . . .
Friend: Yeah. Do you sort of co-ordinate with other people?
Lily: Well, if I did take this job on then I suppose I'd have to, but I'm not sure now whether I want to – do the job, because I, I won't have done that book entirely in my own right, so it's perhaps not worth all the effort. Anyway, translating a whole book, the rate is less than for say, a pharmaceutical article, so I'd probably do better just carrying on as usual, translating articles.
Friend: What about . . . I mean how did you get into it? How did you start translating?
Lily: Oh, having a chat with somebody I was at school with in the pub – they were doing an M.A. on how back problems can be caused by chairs, you know, different sitting positions, and what the best design of a chair would be, for cars and so on, to avoid back problems occurring. And they'd two papers they needed to read but they were in German, so I said that I'd have a go at translating them, and found it was good fun, and carried on from there.
Friend: But you've got qualifications now. Have you done that since?
Lily: Mm, that's since, yes. Well, I started off with a degree and I've also worked in France and Germany for quite some time, so my knowledge of the language was fairly reasonable to start with. And then, when I'd been translating for a couple of years, I, I took a translator's exam, and that qualified me for Associate Membership of the Translator's Guild.

pause

tone
Now you will hear the piece again. [The piece is repeated.]

pause

That is the end of the fourth part of this test.

There will now be a pause to allow you to check your work. The question papers will then be collected by your supervisor.

pause

tone
That is the end of the test.

Practice Test 3

Paper 5: Interview (15–20 minutes)

EMERGENCIES

The following sample package of oral examiner's material enables a complete interview to be given and assessed according to the marking scales given on pages 13 and 14.
  The photographs, passages and activities for Practice Test 3 can be found on pages 116–118 in the Student's Book.

Photographs

Ask the candidate(s) to look at these two photographs. It is Interview Exercise 13 at the back of the Student's Book.

13

Practice Test 3

FAMINE RECOVERY FUND FOR ETHIOPIA AND SUDAN (OXFAM)

Allow a suitable short interval for the candidate(s) to study the photographs and then initiate discussion along these lines:

Describe/compare the scene/activity;
  the possible cause of the situation;
  what the people might be thinking.

Discuss ways of raising money for aid;
  other causes of emergencies.

If a group of two or three candidates is being interviewed, encourage individuals to initiate a discussion on one topic, and invite other candidates to comment.

Passages

Ask the candidate(s) to look at one or more of the passages: Interview Exercises 14, 15 and 16. Invite comment on the content and possible source of the text, who the author or speaker

Practice Test 3

is likely to be, and, where appropriate, what the purpose of the passage is. Comments may also include an expression of agreement or disagreement, interpretation and so on. Candidates must not be encouraged simply to read a whole passage aloud, but may quote from it where this arises naturally during the course of the discussion.

14 After the first week they stopped saying they hoped it would not rain and began to take precautions against fire.
    Grass and bracken were tinder-dry and there had been one or two fires in thatched cottages. On the beaches the sand was blistering to the feet and midday saw only the hardiest of sun-worshippers exposing their bodies. Dustbins and drains were smelling. Milk had turned sour before it was taken from the doorstep. Cases of sunstroke vied with sufferers from sickness and diarrhoea in doctors' surgeries. In the evenings, the air was choked with exhaust fumes as the cars queued to get off the island.

15 A man was critically ill in hospital yesterday after a fire at a chemical plant on Sunday during which toxic gas was released. He was one of three workers in the intensive care unit of the North Tees General Hospital after the incident in which a fertiliser dryer overheated, causing fumes to drift over the St Hilda's area of Middlesbrough. A company spokesman said the cloud was essentially nitrous oxide with traces of hydrochloric acid and ammonia.

16 There were two youngsters standing near me about five or six years old. One of them was bleeding because his face had been cut. I think their father was lying near them. I think he was dead. I helped the little ones climb over the barrier and that was all I could do. Then I fought my way to the front and climbed out myself. It was terrible.

Discussion

Role-play/Discussion

Refer the candidate(s) to the article about defective heaters in Interview Exercise 17 then hand out role cards (the same for each student). Allow the candidate(s) time to absorb the material, then initiate discussion.

Role Card

You work for local T.V. Your team's current assignment is to plan a broadcast warning about the defective Tefal heaters. Discuss details. Points to consider include:

- the length, e.g. 30 seconds, 1 minute, etc.;
- the style and actual content – humorous, serious, cartoon, real-life simulation, any background music, flashing colour, essential information, etc.;
- the time and frequency of transmission – when would most people see it?

17

Defective heaters danger warning

HOUSEHOLDERS should still be aware of some Tefal convector heaters which have been recalled because of a possible wiring defect.

This newspaper warned about the heaters following a statement by Barnet Trading Standards Office before Christmas.

But at least one couple in the borough, who were given a Tefal heater by Barnet Council, used it over Christmas, unaware of the possible danger.

Models 64.47, 64.41, and 64.43 similar to that pictured here should be taken to a Tefal Service Centre for a free adjustment.

The addresses of the Service Centres are available by ringing the Teledata service on 200–0200.

and/or

Discussion

Invite candidate(s) to discuss the topic in Interview Exercise 18:

18 The examiner will ask you to give your views on the following: 'The media are too concerned with disasters. More attention should be paid to less sensational news items.'

Allow a short pause for thought – candidate(s) may make brief notes if they wish.

Practice Test 4

Paper 1: Reading Comprehension (1 hour)

Section A One mark for each correct answer.

1 A	6 D	11 A	16 A	21 A
2 D	7 C	12 D	17 A	22 A
3 B	8 D	13 D	18 D	23 B
4 C	9 D	14 C	19 C	24 A
5 B	10 C	15 B	20 B	25 D

Section B Two marks for each correct answer.

26 C	31 C	36 C
27 B	32 A	37 A
28 D	33 B	38 C
29 C	34 D	39 D
30 A	35 C	40 A

Total: 55

Paper 2: Composition (2 hours)

Give each composition a mark out of 20, according to the scale shown on page 4. If necessary, look at the sample compositions on pages 5–9 for further guidance on the standards required at each grade in the mark scheme.

Total: 40

Paper 3: Use of English (2 hours)

A complete mark scheme is given for each question. The 'raw' total of 69 for this paper would be adjusted to a mark out of 40 in the exam itself. Candidates passing the examination as a whole would be expected to score about 60% of the total marks.

Section A

Question 1 Give one mark for each correct answer.

1 adequate (no alternatives)
2 phrases/pieces/speeches
3 those/stalls
4 would
5 catch
6 out
7 few
8 such

Practice Test 4

9 purpose
10 in/at
11 what/all/everything/anything/whatever
12 that/ensuring (that)
13 gave/offered (**allow** *filled* in 13 with *with* in 14)
14 the/every/great/further/more/some/sufficient (**not** *much*)
15 talk/chat/speak/converse
16 then (no alternatives)
17 my
18 thrown
19 feeling/being
20 case

Total: 20

Question 2

Give one mark for each word or phrase between the vertical lines. Ignore the words printed in italics.

a) *Had his* | aunt not died and | left/given him (a legacy of) £10,000 he would not have been able to buy | *the house he wanted*.

b) *A heavy shower* | put a stop to their game of tennis. |
   | stopped/prevented them (from) finishing their game. |

c) *It was only* | when I saw the photograph (that) I realised he was | *your brother*.

d) *It's* | more than a year / over a year since I went to / since I've been to see them. |

e) *There is* | no statesman (that/who/whom) I admire more than | *the President*.

f) *Don't you get fed* | up (with) (**not** *of*) having to stay / staying / being at home / not going out more / not getting out more | *in the evenings?*

g) *Bob denied* | (that) he had taken / taking / having taken my car. |

h) *Nobody* | is to blame / is responsible for | the fact that the meeting was cancelled / the cancellation of the meeting / the meeting being cancelled. |

Total: 10

Question 3

Give one mark for each word or phrase between the vertical lines. Ignore the words printed in italics.

a) *The man was* | sentenced | *to ten years in prison*.

b) *She'll never learn to play the piano,* | in spite of/despite the number of / no matter how many / however many | *hours she practises*.

c) *You'd better* | pull your | socks up or you'll fail the exam.

d) *They all turned up at the meeting, with* | the exception of | *the treasurer, who was ill*.

59

Practice Test 4

e) *It's hard at first when you become widowed, but people eventually* | get used to / get accustomed to living/being / manage to live / manage to cope with living / come to terms with living | *alone.*

f) | This is one of the worst/best/most (any acceptable adj.) books/newspapers (any acceptable noun) I have ever read. |

Total: 6

Question 4

Give one mark for each word or phrase between the vertical lines, or two marks where shown. Ignore the words printed in italics.

a) | Olsen's recent defeat is/was/dealt a blow to his chance(s) of becoming champion. |
   | Olsen's recent defeat means he is likely to blow his chance(s) of becoming champion. |
   (2 marks or nothing)

b) | It's not worth (the time) trying to explain anything to Tony. |

c) | Nearly/almost/virtually everybody considers stealing to be wrong. |
   | Stealing is considered to be wrong by almost everybody. |

d) | If you don't stand up to him you'll regret it. |
   | Stand up to him and you won't regret it. |
   | Stand up to him or you'll regret it. |
   | You'll regret it unless you stand up to him. |

e) | Lectures are optional for final year students. |
   | Attendance at lectures for final year students is optional. |

f) | I'd/would/should be grateful if you'd/would/could send me / to be sent / if I could be sent further details | *of the job advertised.*

g) *The critic* | did not think much of the new play. |
               | didn't like the new play very much. | (2 marks)

h) | Mary will hardly want to see Christopher in the circumstances. |
   | It is hardly likely that Mary will want . . . |
   | I hardly think Mary will want . . . |
   | I can hardly believe Mary will want . . . |

Total: 10

Section B

Question 5

Give the mark shown for each question for coherent and relevant answers, not necessarily echoing the wording given here.

a) Something in the armed forces / a soldier / fighter.   1

b) To find out where / to look for. . .   1

Practice Test 4

c) Absolutely determined to do something / intent on ...
(answers must carry the idea of emphasis/determination).   1

d) Difficult to travel in USSR (1) and prisoners-of-war were being sent back to USSR (1).   2

e) Paradise/Utopia.   1

f) Had never had/seen them before / something completely new (any one of these for 1 mark).   1

g) Frontier of USSR / between USSR and Estonia / the paradise of the workers.   1

h) Because they were being sent back to the army / had lost their bicycles / had been deceived (any one of these for 1 mark).   1

i) Usually used for animals/cattle (*or*) being treated like animals / dirty and smelly.
(Do not accept *vague* references to bad/uncomfortable conditions.)   1

j) Scarce in times of war/hard to get/buy/find (idea of starvation not enough).   1

k) That it would be almost impossible (Herculean nature of labour) to find two people in such a vast country (any appropriate answer which conveys the enormity of his father's task). (Lifting/quoting of 'Herculean etc ...' without any gloss: 1 mark.)   2

l) Award a maximum of 5 marks for selection of relevant points, i.e.:

   many people wanting to leave Russia
   a recent Revolution
   fighting against Poles
   property confiscated
   food shortages
   people forced into Red Army
   travelling was difficult.   5

Award a maximum of 5 marks for ability to construct a well-written paragraph as opposed to a mere list as this summary is fairly easy. Reward candidates who show evidence of having given some thought to:
– overall construction
– use of connectors
– economical style appropriate to a summary
– some indication of own vocabulary, as opposed to total reliance on lifting.   5

Total: 23

Paper 4: Listening Comprehension (about 30 minutes)

First part: The Muddles

	Score
1 one/1	½
2 one/1	½
3 12 miles	given
4 not given [must be written] (cf 10 & 15)	½
5 design engineer [**no** alternatives, both words necessary]	½

Practice Test 4

6 three/3 — ½
7 one/1 — ½
8 about 200 miles — ½
9 not (too) often/twice a year etc. — ½
10 not given — ½
11 no/none [a dash or stroke to show none can be accepted] — ½
12 two/2 — ½
13 near/round/around (the) corner/not (very) far (away) — ½
14 nearly every day/[**not** everyday/not quite everyday] almost everyday — ½
15 not given — ½

Total: 7 marks

Second part: The Super-Intelligent Machine

Score
16 D 1
17 C 1
18 A 1
19 D 1
20 C 1
21 A 1

Total: 6 marks

Third part: Ex-farmer in service

Score
22 D 1
23 B 1
24 D 1
25 A 1

Total: 4 marks

Fourth part: Museum announcement

Score
26 C 1
27 A 1
28 A 1

Total: 3 marks

Transcript

This is the Certificate of Proficiency Listening Comprehension Test.
Test Number 4
You will be given a question paper for the Certificate of Proficiency Test 4. Your supervisor will give

you further instructions. On the question paper you will see spaces for your name and index number, and questions for each part of the test. Each part of the test will be heard twice. There will be pauses to allow you to look through the questions before each part, and other pauses to let you think about your answers. At the end of every pause you will hear this sound.

tone

The tape will now be stopped while question papers are given out. You must ask any questions now, as you will not be allowed to speak during the test.

pause

First part
You will hear a couple called Mr and Mrs Muddle talking about their children and grandchildren. As you listen, answer questions 1 to 15. If the information is not given, write 'not given' beside the question. You will hear the piece twice.

pause

tone

THE MUDDLES

Interviewer: Mr and Mrs Muddle, I believe you've lived in this area for over thirty years.
Mr Muddle: Oh that's right. (*Yes, that's right.*)
Interviewer: And you have quite a large family, haven't you?
Mr Muddle: Oh yes. My name is Walter Muddle and my wife here's name is Daisy.
Mrs Muddle: And we have three children, one boy and two girls.
Mr Muddle: Well you'd hardly call them children now. They're all grown up, married.
Mrs Muddle: We've got eight grandchildren.
Mr Muddle: Yes, we have a son. He's got two children, a boy of sixteen and a girl of twelve. Now they live not too far away from here, about twelve miles, which is Ashtead in Surrey. And he's a design engineer for a big water company and he travels abroad quite a bit, and his son, he goes to ... what's the name of the school? (*Oh dear.*) I can't remember the name of the school, but he's doing quite well.
Mrs Muddle: We have a daughter lives in Devon, and she has four children.
Mr Muddle: Yes. She has three boys and a little girl. Her husband is a (*He's a policeman, isn't he?*) policeman, and we don't see them too often because they are about two hundred miles away and it is a bit of a long jaunt down there, but we see them perhaps twice a year. And, er, we have another daughter, Jennifer, who lives around the corner from us and she has two daughters, one sixteen and the other one is twelve. They're both at school, of course. And they've just purchased a small dog which gives no end of pleasure to all and sundry.
Mrs Muddle: We wish we could see them more often, the children (*Oh yes, yes.*). We see these, we see those who live round the corner not quite every day, but nearly, you know, but the ones that live in Devon, well we rather wish we could see them more often than we do.
Interviewer: I'm sure you do.

pause

tone
Now you will hear the piece again. [The piece is repeated.]

Practice Test 4

pause

That is the end of the first part of the test.

pause

Second part
You will hear an interview with a man who has written a book about computers. For questions 16 to 21 tick one of the boxes A, B, C or D to show the correct answer. You will hear the piece twice.

pause

tone

THE SUPER-INTELLIGENT MACHINE

Presenter:	We remember how they began only yesterday; they could do arithmetic faster than we could; later they learnt to play games against us – chess, backgammon, that sort of thing. Now they are a long way ahead of such simple achievements. But could they really become more intelligent than we are? Will they take over from us? They, of course, are computers and an attempt to answer these newly urgent questions is made by a science journalist, Adrian Berry, in a book he calls *The Super-Intelligent Machine*. Martin Redfern asked him about the comparison that's made between a computer and human intelligence. Is it, in the first place, a fair comparison?
Adrian Berry:	That is what everyone is trying to do – to try and make it appear to think like a human but in fact, um, show a much more powerful mind. And it already has great advantages, tremendous speed and accuracy, which humans don't have.
Martin Redfern:	Is there any direct way that it can be compared to a human brain, though, in terms of its capabilities or capacity?
Adrian Berry:	Not yet, no. At the moment, um, a computer is rigidly logical and a, a human brain, um, ... all the different parts of the brain are interconnected, whereas with the machine when you use it you only go to, um, one part of it, one tiny part.
Martin Redfern:	A sort of pigeon-holing system?
Adrian Berry:	It has a kind of pigeon-hole mind, and a human brain has a much more – I don't quite know how to say this – a mind in connection with itself.
Martin Redfern:	How do the number of pigeon-holes – the extent of the memory in modern computers – compare with the memory ability, though, of a human brain?
Adrian Berry:	Well, the most powerful computer in the world, which is now the CRAY-1, an American machine, has I think it's the equivalent of six million nerve cells in its brain, whereas the human brain has about ten thousand million.
Martin Redfern:	So computers have got a long way to go yet?
Adrian Berry:	Yes, they have – but they are making very great strides!
Martin Redfern:	And in your book you do make some very striking predictions for the direction in which those strides will take computers and machines – not least the rather ominous direction of the sort of computer which controls its master, which can't be switched off, and which could even attack its programmer.

Practice Test 4

Adrian Berry: This is a possibility that some people might be foolish enough to, um, instruct their computer to be prepared to defend itself against an attack, and it might regard an attempt to switch it off as an attack which it could retaliate against. I'm not saying that people would willingly design such a machine, which would be very dangerous, but they could do it without intending to.

Martin Redfern: Now, in the final chapter of the book you go on to talk about the possibility of computer-based machines colonising planets and taking over the universe.

Adrian Berry: Well, taking over a lot of the colonisation of space, yes. Er, this is in fact the most intelligent way of actually colonising space. If you could have a machine that went on in front of you, and, using local materials, started to construct a moon-base, it would do it immeasurably faster than humans could do it, and then it could also construct another computer identical to itself which could then go off to other planets and do the same thing there. And by spreading in this way, er, within a relatively short time – of a few tens of thousands of years – you could have colonised large parts of the galaxy.

Martin Redfern: Do you really think though, that in the long term, computers will either pose a serious threat to the human race or, as that implies, possibly outlive us?

Adrian Berry: I think the latter. I think it's much more likely that they will be our successor, er, probably biological intelligence has reached the limit of its possible evolution and the next step is electronic intelligence.

Martin Redfern: A lot of people nowadays have computers, even just little personal computers, and one sometimes gets the impression that the computer is the master rather than the person programming it. Is that really the case?

Adrian Berry: Well, there, there's ... it's introduced a lot of pressure into families. Some wives complain that they are neglected by the husband for the sake of the machine. There is actually an agency, a legal agency, in America, which specialises in divorce proceedings, where the computer is, is the co-respondent – and it's actually quite a serious social problem.

pause

tone
Now you will hear the piece again. [*The piece is repeated.*]

pause

That is the end of the second part of the test.

pause

Third part
You will hear an interview with a man who used to be a farmer. For questions 22 to 25 tick one of the boxes A, B, C or D to show the correct answer. You will hear the piece twice.

pause

tone

Practice Test 4

EX-FARMER IN SERVICE

Interviewer: How long have you been in farming?
Ex-Farmer: Well all my life really. My father was farming before me, I was born into it, you see, up the farm, up the top layer where I was born and I . . . I started with my father when I left school. Then shortly after my brother got married. Er, my brother and myself set up in partnership together, you see and that was in 1956, yes, yes and now, now we've ended our partnership. His son has come in with him and, well I've retired. There was a lot wanted doing to the farm, I didn't see it as a, as a feasible investment, you see, for me at my time of life with my family as they are, as it were.
Interviewer: Were there lots of changes in farming?
Ex-Farmer: Well, we made quite a lot of changes, didn't we, yes, yes we brought the farm up to date in our time, but things moved on and then we well we got out-of-date you see. We, we were all hay, it was a very steep farm so it was very side liney, very difficult to get modernised with heavy silage equipment which is what it will have to come to now, yes – because you can't rely that well on the weather you see – and, er, fuel and that for drying is getting more and more expensive and the, the dairy was doubled in my time there and it'll probably increase again now.
Interviewer: And are you enjoying the change from farming now?
Ex-Farmer: Oh yes, yes I am, I am, I am enjoying the changes. It's completely different to anything I've ever experienced before. Now you see I'm in engineering with a neighbour and from, er, 8 in the morning to 5 at night, well, seems a very short day to whatever I was doing before.
Interviewer: Yes. Are there any things that you particularly miss about farming?
Ex-Farmer: Oh well, you miss the cattle don't you, yes, the smell, the fields and you also miss the weather – the last few days, well it's been batting down with rain, innit, so it's not all advantage getting out and it's not all advantage going in, no, no, no, not by a long way. You, er, got to look ahead with farming, a long way ahead, whereas with, with engineering, well, well you don't look so far ahead especially in what I've been doing but, er, so long as you've got a job looked out for when it's raining well you're alright, ain't you?

pause

tone
Now you will hear the piece again. [The piece is repeated.]

pause

That is the end of the third part of the test.

pause

Fourth part
You will hear an announcement about facilities available in a Science Museum. For questions 26 to 28 tick one of the boxes A, B, C or D to show the correct answer. You will hear the piece twice.

pause

tone

Practice Test 4

MUSEUM ANNOUNCEMENT

You will find the museum much more interesting if you listen to the recorded commentaries which supplement the captions on the exhibits. Suitable sound transmitting equipment may be bought from the catalogue stall for £1.50. This equipment remains your property and can be used on future visits.

Museographs are also available for some of the exhibits. These take the form of duplicated sheets, which describe the exhibits in detail and provide historical background, technical information and a bibliography. Museographs are sold at a nominal price from 6 pence upwards, depending on the number of pages. Other leaflets of a more general nature are also available at the catalogue stall, together with postcards and other illustrations.

pause

tone
Now you will hear the piece again. [The piece is repeated.]

pause

That is the end of the fourth part of this test.

There will now be a pause to allow you to check your work. The question papers will then be collected by your supervisor.

pause

tone
That is the end of the test.

Paper 5: Interview (15–20 minutes)

ANIMAL WELFARE

The following sample package of oral examiner's material enables a complete interview to be given and assessed according to the marking scales given on pages 13 and 14.

The photographs, passages and activities for Practice Test 4 can be found on pages 119–121 in the Student's Book.

Practice Test 4

Photographs

Ask the candidate(s) to look at these two photographs. It is Interview Exercise 19 at the back of the Student's Book.

19

Practice Test 4

Allow a suitable short interval for the candidate(s) to study the photographs and then initiate discussion along these lines:

Describe/compare the people/objects;
        the scenes;
        the reason for the demonstration/purpose of the shop.
Discuss the protection of the animal world;
        the usefulness of the animal world;
        attitudes towards animals.

If a group of two or three candidates is being interviewed, encourage individuals to initiate a discussion on one topic, and invite other candidates to comment.

Passages

Ask the candidate(s) to look at one or more of the passages: Interview Exercises 20, 21 and 22. Invite comment on the content and possible source of the text, who the author or speaker is likely to be, and, where appropriate, what the purpose of the passage is. Comments may also include an expression of agreement or disagreement, interpretation and so on. Candidates must not be encouraged simply to read a whole passage aloud, but may quote from it where this arises naturally during the course of the discussion.

20 White-tailed sea eagles have bred successfully in Scotland for the second year running according to the Royal Society for the Protection of Birds. Under the Sea Eagle Project, a pair, which bred last year, have successfully raised two chicks. The birds, which first attempted to breed in 1983, have been guarded round the clock by wardens at a secret nest site.

21 DRIVE OR WALK AROUND

Come and roam around Britain's greatest open zoo. Take a train across the 'Asian Plains' and wander round the 'African Veld'. You'll see some of the world's rarest animals, from majestic tigers to the near-extinct Przewalski's wild horses. Look out for the famous herd of white rhinos. Be sure to see the cheetahs which have bred so well.

22 During the summer a profusion of wild plants produce seed which is the winter food for the ducks and swans which are attracted to the marshy ground. Usually there is sufficiently deep water for diving ducks such as pochard, while large areas which are scarcely covered by water are favoured by enormous flocks of birds such as teal and mallard. Swans swim majestically on the wide areas of shallow lakes, while plovers and waders find food on the high land and near the waters' edge.

Practice Test 4

Discussion

Refer the candidate(s) to the leaflet about London Zoo. Allow them time to absorb the material, then initiate a discussion – 'Zoos should be banned'. The following prompts may be used:

– differences between animals in captivity and pets;
– differences between zoos and safari parks;
– reasons for and against keeping animals in zoos etc.;
– zoos and the preservation of the species.

23 LONDON ZOO
Everybody's zooing it!

SO MUCH TO DO . . .

More than 8,000 animals live at London Zoo. Bongos, bush-babies, bats and boas – come for a day and meet them all. Get nose-to-nose with a tiger. See the giant panda munching bamboo. Walk with a baby elephant. Chat with a mynah. Call in on the scorpions. Look at the night prowlers in the Moonlight World.

On fine days from Easter to the end of September, ride a camel, pony or donkey; take a spin in the pony or llama traps. Join the elephants' weighing and bath time. Meet the animals at their afternoon show.

There are cafés, a restaurant, kiosks and bars for lunches, teas and in-between snacks – souvenirs and films from the Zoo Shop – pushchairs and wheelchairs for hire.

. . . MORE THAN JUST A DAY OUT

FEEDING TIMES

All year, enjoy the animal feeding times – Pelicans and Penguins every afternoon, and Sealions every afternoon but Fridays (when their pond is cleaned). And there's a special feed on Fridays only for the snakes, alligators and lizards in the Reptile House.

OTHER EVENTS All year through, the cows are milked at 3 pm in Children's Zoo. And from Easter to September, there's all the fun of the elephants' weighing and bathtime, and the chance to meet some of the baby animals and their keepers at the 'Meet the Animals' show each afternoon.

OPENING HOURS

London Zoo is open every day of the year except Christmas Day.

and/or

Ask the candidate(s) to look at Interview Exercise 24.

24 The examiner will ask you to speak either for or against the following motion: 'It is folly to concern ourselves with the welfare of animals while our fellow human beings need our help.' You may like to think about the following points when preparing your speech:
- animals are sentient creatures like humans;
- man cannot survive without animals;
- what legacy we leave to further generations;
- exploitation of animals for benefit of humans (e.g. medical research);
- resources devoted to animals not available for human victims of hardship.

Invite the candidate(s) to speak either for or against the motion, using the prompts to guide them in the preparation of the speech(es).

Practice Test 5

Paper 1: Reading Comprehension (1 hour)

Section A One mark for each correct answer.

1 C	6 B	11 A	16 B	21 D
2 D	7 A	12 D	17 A	22 A
3 D	8 D	13 C	18 C	23 C
4 D	9 A	14 B	19 C	24 B
5 B	10 B	15 C	20 C	25 D

Section B Two marks for each correct answer.

26 B	31 D	36 C
27 C	32 B	37 D
28 C	33 C	38 A
29 A	34 B	39 B
30 B	35 D	40 A

Total: 55

Paper 2: Composition (2 hours)

Give each composition a mark out of 20, according to the scale shown on page 4. If necessary, look at the sample compositions on pages 5–9 for further guidance on the standards required at each grade in the mark scheme.

Total: 40

Paper 3: Use of English (2 hours)

A complete mark scheme is given for each question. The 'raw' total of 81 for this paper would be adjusted to a mark out of 40 in the exam itself. Candidates passing the examination as a whole would be expected to score about 60% of the total marks.

Section A

Question 1   Give one mark for each correct answer.

1 by
2 being (no variation – nv)
3 according
4 to

5 others (**allow** some)
6 up
7 bit/little/lot (**not** stage, phase etc.)
8 just/much/rather (**allow** as)
9 latter/adolescent/teenager
10 who (**not** that)
11 had (**allow** has + and appropriate adverb e.g. normally/happily etc.)
12 same
13 be/pose/present/become/cause
14 when/where
15 over (**not** upon)
16 a
17 looks/searches/seeks/longs (no further variations – nfv)
18 which (**allow** order)
19 reached (nv)
20 not (nv)

Total: 20

Question 2

Give one mark for each word or phrase between the vertical lines. Ignore the words printed in italics.

a) *The students regretted not* | attending / going to / having attended / having gone to |

   the lecture.

b) *Unless you* | saw / heard / listened to / watched / have seen etc. |

   the programme you can't really judge.

c) *It is* | (now) twenty years since J and M moved (**not** have moved)

   (**allow** twenty years ago that J and M moved) | *to Edinburgh.*

d) *However* | hard she works (may/might work) | *she never seems to succeed.*

e) *It was not so* | much a discussion | as an argument. |

f) *Hardly* | a day passes/goes by (**allow** any day) without me/my writing | *to him.*
           but I write
           when I don't write

g) *Mary reported* | the burglary to the police. |

h) *I never had* | any (**allow** *the* only with *slightest*) intention | of going | *to the meeting.*

(Second mark not dependent on first.)

Total: 10

Practice Test 5

Question 3

Give one mark for each word or phrase between the vertical lines. Ignore the words printed in italics.

a) *On no occasion since then* | has/had she acted/gone | *against her mother's wishes*.

b) *You* | couldn't/can't/mustn't have won/got | *the prize or you'd have heard by now*.
　　　　　didn't win/get
　　　　　haven't won/got

c) *It's dark! Mind* | (that) you don't/she doesn't/etc. | *get lost!* (**allow** acceptable variants, e.g. Mind (out for) the cars and don't get lost.)

d) *He didn't take kindly* | to being | *criticised*.

e) *He likes nothing* | better/more/other than | *to sit and read the daily paper*.
　　　　　　　　　　else but

f) *It must be twenty-five years* | (any correct addition with since/ago/when + simple past) | *at school*.

Total: 6

Question 4

Give one mark for each word or phrase between the vertical lines. Ignore the words printed in italics.

a) | Dickens died without finishing his last novel |
　　　　　　　　　　　　 having finished . . .
　　　　　　　　　　　　 being able to finish etc. |

b) | The kidnappers let all the hostages go/leave | *yesterday*.

c) | It came as a shock/surprise | *to hear that he had failed his driving test*.

d) | He expressed (his) disapproval of | *people who smoked*.

e) | In all probability he will come/is coming.
　　 There is a high/distinct/strong (**not** good/great)
　　　　probability that he will come/of his coming. |

f) | What caused the explosion is still unknown.
　　 It is unknown/not known / Nobody knows what caused the explosion. |
　　 (**not** awkward variants such as: It is still unknown by what the explosion was caused.)

g) | The defendant was (sentenced to be) jailed for 6 months.
　　 The judge jailed the defendant / sentenced the defendant to be jailed for 6 months. |
　　 (No marks if 'in/to' included.)

h) | It never occurred to me (ignore *has*) | to go by train/that I could go by train. |
　　 | (The thought of) going by train | never occurred to me. |

Total: 9

Practice Test 5

Section B

Question 5

Give the mark shown for each question for coherent and relevant answers, not necessarily echoing the wording given here.

a) (Any idea/statement of a fish blocking a harbour.)   1

b) 'Sardine' was the name of a boat (1) used to block the harbour during the Revolution (1). 2

c) Insurgents – generalised explanation of rebels/revolutionaries etc. (**not** just 'opponents of counter revolutionaries')   1

d) People forget the details (1). People are not interested in historical fact (1). People prefer good stories to real facts (1).   3

e) They believe a fish blocked the harbour (1) because they exaggerate/enjoy jokes (1).   2

f) The people of Marseille exaggerate the truth (1). They are also fond of tricking people (1).   2

g) Out-of-season – not in April / at a different time of year (1). April foolery – playing tricks/practical jokes (1).   2

h) (Any reference to comparative size of baby and adult.)   1

i) Separated from its companions (1). Died of thirst/starvation/natural causes (1).   2

j) One month (1). The smell from the carcase (1).   2

k) The sheer size of the animal.   1

l) An acceptable expression of:
    a sense of wonder – the amazing animal (1)
    a feeling of sorrow and sympathy for the animal, treated so roughly in death (1)
    self-loathing – enjoying a spectacle of death (1).
    (allow lifting)   3

m) A following event / the next act in the drama.   1

n) Both stories are:
    about a sea creature (of real/exaggerated size) (1)
    about blocking a main route in Marseille (1)
    This story of the whale will be exaggerated/become a legend like the story of the sardine (1).   3

o) Award 5 marks for content covering the following information:

    the background details – any two out of type/size/age/weight
    the causes of death
    the tongue and the traffic jam
    used for cosmetics
    will become a legend   5

In addition, award up to 5 marks for:
– concise, coherent writing
– good command of paragraph structure
– connected summary   5

Practice Test 5

Penalise:
– rambling
– irrelevant lifting
Use the scale: 5 – fluent and confidently correct
                3 – reasonably fluent
                0 – poor, unconnected

Total: 36

Paper 4: Listening Comprehension (about 30 minutes)

First part: *The dog*

		Score
1	F	½
2	F	½
3	F	½
4	F	½
5	T	½
6	T	½

Total: 3 marks

Second part: *Doctor's chair*

		Score
7	B	1
8	C	1
9	A	1
10	D	1
11	A	1

Total: 5 marks

Third part: *Edinburgh Leisure Line*

		Score
12	dolls and figures/dolls/figures	½
13	10 a.m.	½
14	Bridge/bridge (just off Princes Street)	½
15	554 4494	½
16	Royal Mile/royal mile	½
17	300/three hundred	½
18	15/fifteen	½
19	31	½
20	theatre	½
21	country	½

Total: 5 marks

Practice Test 5

Fourth part: Studio management problems

		Score
22	D	1
23	C	1
24	D	1
25	C	1
26	A	1
27	A	1
28	C	1

Total: 7 marks

Transcript

This is the Certificate of Proficiency Listening Comprehension Test.
Test Number 5
You will be given a question paper for the Certificate of Proficiency Test 5. Your supervisor will give you further instructions. On the question paper you will see spaces for your name and index number, and questions for each part of the test. Each part of the test will be heard twice. There will be pauses to allow you to look through the questions before each part, and other pauses to let you think about your answers. At the end of every pause you will hear this sound.

tone

The tape will now be stopped while question papers are given out. You must ask any questions now, as you will not be allowed to speak during the test.

pause

First part
You will hear a conversation about keeping animals as pets. For questions 1–6 tick one box to show whether the statement is true or false. You will hear the piece twice.

pause

tone

THE DOG

Interviewer: I notice you've got a dog – quite a large dog . . .
Man: Difficult *not* to notice . . .
Woman: Well, it's not actually my dog; it's actually my husband's dog, I mean I simply put up with it . . . or *not* as the case may be.
Interviewer: I gather from that that you don't really like it.
Woman: No, if it was up to me I wouldn't have any animals at all, because I don't really like having pets or animals in the house, um, you know, it seems a shame that, you know if one's husband and son shouldn't have pets if they want them so, as I say, I put up with them.
Interviewer: What is it you don't like about having pets around?
Woman: Oh, well partly the mess and the dirt and the hairs everywhere not that he is particularly bad, but any animal introduces hairs and mess into the house. I

77

Practice Test 5

	mean he comes back from walks you know all muddy and gets mud all over the floor and clothes, and that sort of thing and partly that, er, well you can't ignore him because he's much too large to ignore and he's also – well, he's very affectionate. Yes he's very friendly, aren't you? And he comes running up when you come back if you've been out, and, you know, wants lots of attention, which I find infuriating because I don't really like animals. I don't want him here. I don't want to have to respond to him, you know, pet him and pat him on the head you know ...
Man:	You don't like dogs because they're parasites because ...
Woman:	Yes I know. I much prefer cats in that sense. I wouldn't by choice have a cat anyway but I much prefer a cat to a dog, you know, because they are much more, well they're much more independent, I mean they've got more self respect than dogs. Dogs fawn on you and sort of you know they're completely indiscriminate in that they don't want people to respond to them and they don't seem to differentiate between people who like them and people who don't like them.
Interviewer:	Wouldn't you miss him if he went?
Woman:	Oh, yes. I mean it would be much nicer ...

pause

tone
Now you will hear the piece again. [The piece is repeated.]

pause

That is the end of the first part of the test.

pause

Second part
You will hear part of a radio programme in which an actor is interviewed. For questions 7 to 11 tick one of the boxes A, B, C or D to show which is the correct answer. You will hear the piece twice.

pause

tone

DOCTOR'S CHAIR

Doctor: Good evening, Gary. I may call you that, may I?
Gary: Please do.
Doctor: Well, now, Gary, you've agreed to come and sit in the Patient's Chair, with an audience in the studio, and many thousands of people listening – does this mean that you enjoy being the centre of attention ... that you like talking about yourself in fact?
Gary: I guess I must – I mean I like people around me, and – being an actor, I'm used to being looked at and listened to, I guess.
Doctor: Is that why you took up acting as a profession then? So that you could gain the notice of others?
Gary: Could be ... I suppose ... I hadn't really thought of it that way ...
Doctor: How did you get involved in acting? Is it something that runs in the family?

Gary: No ... I can't say it is ... My kid sister Susan took up dancing but ...
Doctor: As a career you mean?
Gary: It was, yes, but well she's married now – so ...
Doctor: I see. So both you and your younger sister went on stage. Um, what did your parents think of it? Did they encourage you?
Gary: Did they encour ... no, I wouldn't say they encouraged it ...
Doctor: Well, were they actually pleased then to see their son – and I believe you're their only son – taking up something as risky as acting?
Gary: Oh I think my mother was – yeah, I'd say *she* was.
Doctor: You think your mother was pleased?
Gary: Sure, yeah ... We didn't actually talk about it that much, but ...
Doctor: I'll come back to that point if I may. But, first, what about your father? How does he figure in this? And in your early background?
Gary: My father? It's hard to say, really. He'd died of course before I became well-known – so he only saw me in what you might call my struggling years as a young actor – oh that was before I got my first real break with the Royal –
Doctor: You're not really answering my question though, are you? How did you and your father relate to each other? Was the acting business a bone of contention between you perhaps?
Gary: Oh we didn't actually quarrel – exchange words over it – if that's what you're saying. No. It's just that he didn't go along with it – that's all.
Doctor: What would he like – would he have liked – you to become instead?
Gary: Oh, he wanted me to go on to College – University – teach or something.
Doctor: And he *had* been to University himself?
Gary: No ... no he hadn't. He was just a clerk. He worked in a bank from when he left school. He read a lot. I, I think he'd have liked a better education but ...
Doctor: So he wanted it for you?
Gary: Something like that.
Doctor: So you're saying your father didn't want you to follow in his footsteps, but he didn't want you to be an actor either? And did you never – as a young boy perhaps – feel that you wanted to become *like* him in some way?
Gary: No, I didn't.

pause

tone

Now you will hear the piece again. [The piece is repeated.]

pause

That is the end of the second part of the test.

pause

Third part
You will hear a recorded telephone announcement about visiting Edinburgh in Scotland. For questions 12 to 21 fill in the missing information in the gaps provided. You will hear the piece twice.

pause

tone

Practice Test 5

EDINBURGH LEISURE LINE

Welcome to Edinburgh. We have some suggestions for ways in which you may care to spend your days in and around the capital.

One of the most exciting of the festival exhibitions has already opened to the public. More than 100 original dolls and figures made by members of the British Doll Artists' Association are on display at the Cannongate Tollbooth Museum in the Royal Mile. Cannongate Tollbooth is open between 10a.m. and 6p.m.

One of the best ways to see this beautiful and historic city is by joining one of the many coach tours organised by Lothian Region Transport; these tours cover all parts of the city and leave from Waverley Bridge, just off Princes Street, throughout the day. For details telephone 554 4494.

An interesting evening can be enjoyed by all who arrive at the Carlton Hotel at 8p.m. Following a welcoming drink you will be conducted along the Royal Mile, Scotland's most historic thoroughfare, by a member of the Scottish Tours Guides Association. On returning to the hotel you can join in the Scottish entertainment, a ceilidh – for details telephone 556 7277.

Most of Scotland is on Edinburgh's doorstep; you'll be surprised just how much of it you can see in a day. Scottish Omnibuses operate an extensive varied programme of day and afternoon tours every day from the bus station at St Andrew's Square. – Telephone 556 8464.

Edinburgh Zoo has Scotland's largest collection of wild animals and is open between 9a.m. and 6p.m. 365 days a year. The finest colony of penguins in any zoo share a beautiful parkland setting that includes over 300 different species; the zoo is only 15 minutes from the city centre. Buses to and from the zoo are numbers 12, 26, 31 and 86; car parking facilities are also available.

Your entertainment at the Ross Open Air Theatre in Princes Street Gardens begins at 3p.m. with Scottish light music; at 7.30p.m. Alistair Wood and his Scottish country dance band provide the music for Scottish country dancing.

To find out more about events or places of interest to visit please call at the Tourist Information Centre at 5 Waverley Bridge or telephone 226 6591. We do hope you enjoy your day in the capital and thank you for calling.

pause

tone
Now you will hear the piece again. [The piece is repeated.]

pause

That is the end of the third part of the test.

pause

Fourth part
You will hear Abbas talking about his experiences as a studio manager. For questions 22 to 28 tick one of the boxes A, B, C or D to show which is the correct answer. You will hear the piece twice.

pause

tone

STUDIO MANAGEMENT PROBLEMS

Woman: The thing is, I mean the attitude of management makes a lot of difference to how

	people react when they work, (*Mm*) how much, what they're prepared to put into it, and everything like that.
Abbas:	Mm, yes, mm, yes well. Very much the same as that business of where I used to work. Erm, there was, as you know, there was this studio, I used to run the studio. Six, seven people working there, typesetters, photographers, paste-up artists, designers and things (*Yeah*). There were times that I was very busy, with larger projects and things, and I had to give them a job, and say (*Get on with it.*) yeah, get on with it, and start from scratch, organise the typesetting, (*Yeah*) camera, making plates, send it to the printers, check the proofs, check the first pull from the machine (*Yeah*) and, then ...
Woman:	Good heavens, it sounds really hectic.
Abbas:	That would be for three colours, and the customer would want five thousand (*Yeah*). There was a word once, Churchill Garage or Churchill College, I can't remember. Then I said to Barry, said, can you get on with it, and ask Jan to set the Churchill College, and check it, and do the artwork and send it, (*Yeah*) and go through the procedure. And he said, 'Yes,' and came to me half an hour later, and said, 'What was that word?' and I said, 'Churchill College,' and he went again. And near lunchtime I asked him, 'How're you doing Barry?' and he said, 'Oh, er, what was that word?' – 'Oh, God, all right,' – I wrote, in a very panic, and scribbled a bit of, you know, the word Churchill College on a bit of paper and gave it to him, not realising that I'd spelled Churchill with one l (*Uhuh*) instead of two (*Yeah*) and naturally, that's not the sort of mistake I make.
Woman:	Everybody in England knows how to spell Churchill.
Abbas:	Anybody can make a mistake, yes, anybody knows that. The, er, the whole thing went through the procedure and a couple of days later the production manager came to see me and said, 'Do you think the customer will accept this?' I said, 'What's wrong with it?' 'Well, Churchill's got one l!' I said, 'Oh, my God ...'
Woman:	And hadn't he checked it, or anything?
Abbas:	No, 'cause what happened, he, he go, he goes to Jan, and says, 'Can you set this?' and Jan says, 'Oh, Churchill's got one l,' and he said, 'Oh, that's all right, that's what Abbas has written,' (*Mm*) and Jan says, 'Of course, he's made a mistake, OK, but shall we check it with him?' And he says, 'No, no, no, just get on with it, do exactly as he's done it,' (*Yeah*) and, er, so they set Churchill with one l, and it goes through the photography, making plates, three colours and goes through the whole, er, routine. (*Yeah*) And the reason he's done it, is because he was acting against the company, not against me, he didn't have anything against me personally, but because I was representing the company. He thought right, that's just another bit of ...
Woman:	That's their bad luck.
Abbas:	That's their bad luck. Yeah.
Woman:	I mean, didn't he know, or did he just not care, do you think?
Abbas:	No, he didn't care, he definitely knew how to spell Churchill College, specially after Jan told him, (*Yeah*) and, er, but he just didn't care. He thought, well, that'll, you know, cause a bit more damage to the firm.

pause

tone
Now you will hear the piece again. [*The piece is repeated.*]

pause

Practice Test 5

That is the end of the fourth part of this test.

There will now be a pause to allow you to check your work. The question papers will then be collected by your supervisor.

pause

tone
This is the end of the test.

Paper 5: Interview (15–20 minutes)

MONARCHY AND GOVERNMENT

The following sample package of oral examiner's material enables a complete interview to be given and assessed according to the marking scales given on pages 13 and 14.
    The photographs, passages and activities for Practice Test 5 can be found on pages 122–124 in the Student's Book.

Photographs

Ask the candidate(s) to look at the photographs below. It is Interview Exercise 25 at the back of the Student's Book.

25

THE YWCA
OF GREAT BRITAIN
This plaque was unveiled by
HER MAJESTY
THE QUEEN
on 21st March 1985 to mar
the official reopening of
HELEN GRAHAM
HOUSE

Practice Test 5

Allow a suitable short interval for candidate(s) to study the photographs and then initiate discussion along these lines:

Describe/compare the people;
                 the setting;
                 the activity.

Discuss the interest shown in monarchy;
          the reasons for the survival of monarchy;
          the alternatives to monarchy.

If a group of two or three candidates is being interviewed, encourage individuals to initiate a discussion on one topic, and invite other candidates to comment.

Passages

Ask the candidate(s) to look at one or more of the passages: Interview Exercises 26, 27 and 28. Invite comment on the content and possible source of the text, who the author or speaker is likely to be, and, where appropriate, what the purpose of the passage is. Comments may also include an expression of agreement or disagreement, interpretation and so on. Candidates must not be encouraged simply to read a whole passage aloud, but may quote from it where this arises naturally during the course of the discussion.

26   The bride of the year, Miss Sarah Ferguson, entered Westminster Abbey yesterday a commoner, a girl from the shires in a headdress of summer flowers, and emerged glittering with diamonds as Her Royal Highness, The Duchess of York, wife of Prince Andrew, the newly-created Duke of York.

27   BOOK SIX   Which treats of the life, works, and conquests of the Inca Pachacutec, ninth king of Peru. With a description of the royal mansions; of the funeral ceremonies of the kings; of the hunting season; posts and messengers; Empire archives and accounts.

28   PHILADELPHIA/NEW YORK
This morning visit Philadelphia, the home of the First and Second Continental Congresses and first capital of the U.S. Enjoy a brief sightseeing tour of the city before arriving at Independence Hall, site of the signing of the Declaration of Independence and home of the Liberty Bell.

Practice Test 5

Discussion

Ask the candidate(s) to look at the drawing and plan in Interview Exercise 29 and allow them time to study them.

29

The House of Commons during a debate.

Plan of the Chamber of <u>the House of Lords</u> showing the Woolsack and the positions of the Government, Opposition and Cross Benches

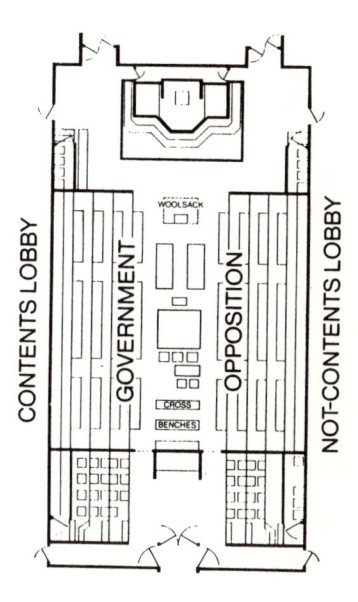

Invite the candidate(s):
– to describe the sytem of government in their own country and/or
– to contrast the system of government in their own country with the system in Britain.

and/or

Invite the candidate(s) to answer one or both of the following questions. Allow a short pause for thought – candidate(s) may make brief notes if they wish.

30
a) What are the biggest changes you would make if you were in charge of the government of your country / of Britain?
b) What do you see as the most difficult problems facing the government in your country / in Britain?

85

Practice Test 5

Paper 5: Interview (15–20 minutes)

Optional Reading

PATRICIA HIGHSMITH: *The Talented Mr Ripley*

The following sample package of oral examiner's material enables a complete interview to be given and assessed according to the marking scales given on pages 13 and 14. The relevant pages in the Student's Book are 125 and 126. A summary is given below for your reference.

Summary

Tom Ripley, unemployed and living in a squalid room in New York, extracts perverted pleasure but no profit from conning people into making tax payments by cheques he cannot cash. He is approached by the father of a slight acquaintance, Dickie Greenleaf, who now lives in Italy, and agrees to attempt to persuade Dickie to return to America.

In Europe his talent for deceit flourishes, and this, together with a total lack of any moral sense and a schizophrenic ability to assume a different persona and 'remember' situations and conversations which have never taken place, enables him to make imaginative and profitable use of every opportunity that presents itself.

He ingratiates himself with Dickie, who paints bad pictures and has an affectionate platonic relationship with Marge Sherwood, another expatriate American. Tom becomes insanely jealous. He kills Dickie, dumps the body in the sea and assumes his identity. He moves to Rome, forges Dickie's signature to avail himself of his monthly remittance from America and writes, as Dickie, convincingly enough to Marge and Greenleaf senior to allay any suspicion.

All is well until a friend, Freddie Miles, turns up and is very suspicious at seeing Tom wearing Dickie's jewellery. Tom kills him without premeditation and prepares a careful story for the police. They appear unsatisfied and enquire about Ripley's whereabouts. The validity of the forged signatures is also questioned. It is time for 'Dickie Greenleaf' to disappear.

Tom reappears as himself in northern Italy. Dickie is now missing and suspected of murder, and Tom initiates the idea that he has committed suicide. He produces an envelope entrusted to him, he says, by Dickie. It contains a will, forged by Ripley, leaving him all Dickie's possessions. When Dickie's clothes and passport are found, the search for him – obviously now dead or living under another name – is called off, and Tom is left imagining how he will spend his 'inheritance'. By his imaginative planning Tom has managed to avoid every pitfall but his life is now as dreary as it was in New York. He actually grieves for Dickie but he has no sense of guilt for his death.

Photograph

You may want an 'ice-breaker' to open the interview, in which case use the illustration in Interview Exercise 31 or:
– a photograph of your own choice, perhaps text-related;
– a copy of the text itself;
– (by prior arrangement with the school etc. concerned) project work by the candidate(s) on the text.

Whichever method is adopted, allow suitable preparation time and initiate conversation as appropriate.

Practice Test 5

31

[Book cover: Patricia Highsmith — THE TALENTED MR RIPLEY, Penguin]

Passages

Ask the candidate(s) to look at one or more of the passages: Interview Exercises 32, 33 and 34. Invite comment on the content etc. as for the general passages in other Interview Exercises, but within the special scope of text-based discussion (identification of character, incident, setting etc. as appropriate). Follow up with discussion of especially enjoyed, typical or unusual features of the text.

32   Tom had never seen them, but he could see them now, precise draughtsman's drawings with every line and bolt and screw labelled, could see Dickie smiling, holding them up for him to look at and he could have gone on for several minutes describing details for Mr Greenleaf's delight, but he checked himself.

Practice Test 5

33 He chose a dark-blue silk tie and knotted it carefully. The suit fitted him. He re-parted his hair and put the parting a little more to one side, the way Dickie wore his.

'Marge, you must understand that I don't *love* you,' Tom said into the mirror in Dickie's voice, with Dickie's higher pitch on the emphasised words.

34 He hated Dickie, because, however he looked at what had happened, his failing had not been his own fault, not due to anything he had done, but due to Dickie's inhuman stubbornness. And his blatant rudeness. He had offered Dickie friendship, companionship and respect, everything he had to offer and Dickie had replied with ingratitude and now hostility.

Discussion

Select one or more of the topics in Interview Exercise 36 for the candidate(s) to discuss.

35 The examiner will ask you to discuss one or more of the following topics:

1 How much does the chief character manipulate the plot?
2 the situation of any one or more characters, in a 'What could he/she have done?' context.
3 reasons for liking or disliking the book.
4 insights into the society and attitudes portrayed.
5 the setting and descriptive background.
6 Could this novel be called a study in madness?
7 What is our attitude to Ripley? Do we want the police to catch up with him?
8 Would this novel make a good film?